Dear Ken + Janet
The lord has ... my life
with friends ... ith
like you. H ... he
awesome things He's been ...... us.

OVERCOMING

In His love,
Ken

Giants
of the
Heart

Ken Hepner

WINEPRESS WP PUBLISHING

ISBN 1-57921-141-0
Library of Congress Catalog Card Number: 98-61040

Dedicated to: six men whom the Lord used as loving tools in His hands, as He was shaping my heart.

Samuel C. Hepner
Kenneth Beasom
M. Eugene Heidler
Owen Alderfer
Henry Ginder
Ray Bert

With deepest appreciation!

Contents

Introduction

Andrea was thirty-three years old, married, and had three children. She came to the church one day in search of help for the awful pain she had in her heart. She realized she was in the process of physically harming her infant son. She was terrified of what could happen if she snapped again and lost all sense of reality. She had been in counseling for several years and had gotten in touch with tremendous wounding she had experienced as a child growing up. When she was a little girl a neighbor man had molested her repeatedly. Her counselor helped her to realize she was angry at this incredible abuse for which she was not in any way responsible. Her anger seemed to be growing since she learned that the perpetrator had died. Now she seemed to be taking the anger out on her husband and infant son in a type of displacement of feelings regarding these wounds inflicted on her by another male.

There had been a growing, almost seething, anger just under the surface for weeks. It came to a head the previous day with the physical abuse she found herself carrying out on her innocent baby boy. As she sat in the office of one of our pastoral staff, she was terrified of what she might do to herself or her son. She didn't want to live with this inner turmoil and wounding of the heart anymore. She came to us as a sort of last-ditch effort to find help. Her maternal instincts caused her to realize that what she had been pondering—suicide—was a better alternative than doing something harmful to her son, whom she loved. Her bottom-line issue was very simple: if we couldn't help her find release from this inner prison of the heart, she was going to bring it to an end herself.

Over the next number of weeks some wonderful sisters in Christ Jesus ministered the grace of God to her. They helped her go back to the horrible places of wounding. But this time, as they explored her abusive past, they walked with her by faith to the cross of our Lord Jesus. There, as she met with Him and confessed the awful wounds of molestation and her helplessness as a young girl to prevent it, Jesus our Lord took the wounds away and destroyed them. She found that inner-healing and release from the bondage of hopelessness brought change in her thoughts. She found healing grace that covered over the multitude of horrible sins done to her. She realized how precious she was to God as His special daughter. The Lord Jesus gave her forgiveness for the offender, which she released in prayer at the foot of the cross with her sisters.

The Lord set her free from the inner wounds and bondage of the heart that held her prisoner for nearly twenty years. All sins are destroyed at the cross of Jesus Christ our Lord, even the ones done to us. Sins committed against us can hold us in an inner-prison of the heart for many years.

Today Andrea is a person who helps other women walk by faith to the Lord Jesus and, at the cross, lay in His bosom the offenses done to them. As Andrea found, the wounded heart finds grace and mercy in His touch, and by His healing grace, the one set free can pursue a lifetime of hunger for the holiness and majesty of God.

Carl was a young pastor in his mid-forties who came to our church one day and asked if I thought we could help him with some internal struggles he had been having for years. He poured out a story that is common of people who grew up in the fifties and sixties. He had an absentee father who worked long, hard hours in order to keep the family fed and clothed. His mom had been physically abused by family members when she was growing up. She was volatile in her anger at Carl and his little brothers. He felt as though he had to shield Bobby and Jimmy from her tirades, and so for most of his childhood and adolescence, he was cursed and cut down by her as "no-good, worthless trash that will never amount to a thing."

Sins committed against us can hold us in an inner-prison of the heart for many years.

Carl became a successful pastor, a good preacher, and his church was doing well. The church was about to begin a building program that should have been somewhat fulfilling. However, with the increased load in schedule and concomitant stress, there was an inner danger he increasingly feared. There was buried frustration and a seething pot of emotion just beneath the surface. The more pressure he was under at the church, the more the anger seemed to well up and require him to deal with it.

Then after his parents died in a car crash, Carl experienced a tremendous increase in these feelings of anger and frustration: it seemed to grow almost overnight following their deaths. Anger began to boil out onto his wife, whom he very much loved and would never want to hurt. She was his sweetheart, yet he found himself speaking harshly and unkindly to her, hurting her soft heart. Even worse, these angry explosions were becoming increasingly frequent in their manifestations. He treated his two teenage daughters with coldness, harshness, and anger over silly things, which he knew very well he should be able to overlook as teenage frivolity. It scared him to think about how angry he was becoming.

Then there was the awful amount of criticism he took at church for being an egomaniac and dictatorial power-hungry man. Very often, building programs are done at the expense of the pastor's integrity, because for some reason, investing money in the Kingdom tends to bring out the worst in some people. The more he was criticized, the more angry he became. He knew very well this out-of-control emotion wasn't the will of God. He did his best to go to the cross of Christ Jesus and lay off the feelings he was experiencing. He had, up to that point, been able to walk in forgiveness for the people of the church who were hurting him. But what he felt toward himself and his own family and what came out of him, were unacceptable to him. He knew it wasn't what the Lord Jesus had made available to him as a child of God.

We walked with Carl for weeks as he unfolded his story of abuse, hurt, heartache, and inner debts of the heart. This time, as he remembered them, we walked with him to the cross of Jesus and he confessed them by faith to the Lord. Little by little, he was being released from the inner prison of anger and frustration. As he watched Jesus take his wounds away one at a time, he began to see a concomitant drop in his frustration and anger level.

The Lord brought him to the place of deep forgiveness for the offenses done to him—the shaming and cursing he had received as a child. As Christ gave him forgiveness for his mom and dad, who had passed away, he was able to confess it to them in prayer with tremendous amounts of deep emotion. As he released them of their having wounded him, he was able to experience a sweet flow of the peace and joy of the Holy Spirit into his heart. Following his final prayer session with the Lord Jesus at the cross, the inner barometric readings of anger and frustration dropped almost at once. The risen Lord Jesus was now standing up tall in the very areas where Carl had been in inner prison cells of fear, anger, and unforgiveness.

The bottom line of these two stories is that, as the people of God, we must first attack the internal issues of the heart before we are ready to attack the external battles for the kingdom of God. We must first experience inner victory in the ground of our own hearts, before we are prepared to put on the full armor of God and help someone else to be set free in His provisions. This book is about factors the Lord has taught us about healing the inner wounds and debts of the heart. We will be referring to these as "inner giants of the heart." This book is written to encourage us to walk in the provisions our Lord Jesus died to give us and that we might walk in an ever-increasing awareness of His holiness and majesty. The price He paid and the love He extends to us by His Spirit must be received personally and experientially.

The theological perspective from which I am writing is Wesleyan/Armenian. This is, in a nutshell, a theology that addresses the heart of the believer. The Lord God desires for us as His sons and daughters to be holy. This is not merely positional holiness, but also personal and relational. His desire is for us to walk by faith with Him to the cross and choose to appropriate His death for us regarding our sins, the sinful desires that are in us by reason of our humanity, and the world's allure to us. He desires to remove footholds, or strongholds, the enemy has been permitted to construct in us over time. This is deeply personal and experiential and is done for us by God at our invitation and at the point of surrender of our will.

> **. . . we must first attack the internal issues of the heart before we are ready to attack the external battles for the kingdom of God.**

The Word of the Lord is a mighty weapon. The Lord Jesus said, "You shall know the truth and the truth will set you free." He prayed to the Father, "Sanctify them by the truth; your word is truth." His Word is both general and personal revelation, because the Author lives in us as Counselor. God's truth must be believed and confessed through lips of faith. The place to begin is in the internal battlefield of the heart. Are you a person with a hunger to be a spiritual overcomer? Let's study the issue with a view to being children of God—children who are walking in His provisions of holiness and spiritual victory!

Part One

Issues of the Heart

Chapter One

Healing the Warrior's
Wounded Heart

IN THE WORD OF GOD, we are called to live our lives
here on planet earth as people who have been given spiritual authority to walk as warriors of the faith. We are given
hundreds of biblical pictures of our calling to be spiritual
victors in Christ Jesus. This concept of being spiritual overcomers is, in reality, an issue of walking by faith in the victory of Christ Jesus. It's not something we can do for ourselves; we are wholly dependent upon Him to give it to us.
The Scriptures make it abundantly clear that He Himself is
our victory! He came to earth to bring us eternal life and
the gift of righteousness—now. He came to destroy the
devil's power over us and to set us free from the inner chains
that bind us—chains of the heart and mind. Our walking
in spiritual victory is, therefore, primarily an issue of being

in ever-deepening relationship with the Lord Jesus by His indwelling Holy Spirit:

> The thief comes only to steal and kill and destroy. I have come that they might have life and have it to the full. (John 10:10)

> [Jesus] replied, "I saw Satan fall like lightning from heaven. I have given you authority to trample on snakes and scorpions and to overcome all the power of the enemy. However, do not rejoice that the spirits are subject to you, but rejoice that your names are written in heaven." (Luke 10:18–20)

From those, and countless other Scriptures, we learn the tremendous truth with which every child of God must come to grips on a personal level. Our Lord Jesus came and destroyed the devil's power by defeating sin, the flesh nature, the world's allure to us, and spiritual beings of darkness in order that Christ might rule over us. Because of who He is and what He has done for us, we do not have to live with sin, bondage, or inner heartache. In Him through faith, we have been given back the ground of our hearts and lives. It is a matter of appropriating by faith His Word of truth, which sets us free. One of my life verses is Romans 5:17:

> For if by the trespass of the one man death reigned through the one man, how much more will those who receive God's abundant provisions of grace and the gift of righteousness *reign in life through the one man Jesus Christ.* (emphasis mine)

To some it may be too simplistic to decide that something is the will of God; therefore, I choose to live like this—with the attitude of an overcomer. It may appear on the surface to be simply a matter of choice. Without question, it is true that we are called to live as spiritual overcomers by faith, and He must be taken at His Word. Yet, life isn't quite that simple. Choosing to appropriate His provision by faith isn't always that easily accomplished by some of His special sons and daughters. Sometimes there are tremendous inner roadblocks of the heart that stand in the way of our being able to see, let alone stand in His truth and to appropriate it by faith.

Throughout this book we'll be referring to these roadblocks as inner giants of hopelessness, despair, and discouragement. These are rooted in wounds and heartaches of the past—painful memories buried in the subconscious mind. This book is about the decision many of us as God's children need to make to face, one by one, those inner issues that block our walk in His provision of spiritual victory. This book is written from the perspective of helping us to see and appropriate His spiritual victory deeply in our hearts. It is written to help us attack inner giant-sized issues created by painful memories, which perhaps have not been faced for many years, let alone dealt with in His provision for us at the cross!

One of the things the Lord has made crystal-clear to me as I have loved and ministered to people, is that life is sometimes hard and cruel. There are few people who have escaped being wounded in the mind, heart, and soul. Most people, whom you meet at your workplace or on Sunday morning in your church, have experienced the reality that sometimes life is hard. Wounds occur in the best families—

in the very places where children are to experience security and come to know something of the Father God's heart of love.

In a child's life, there can be the dichotomy of pain and love flowing from the same person. This is hard for an adult to understand, let alone a child or a teenager. Often those wounds of the heart are not really addressed or dealt with at any depth. They are more or less glossed over, and the wounded heart is left to create a rationale for why it's not so bad, and to learn to cope with the hurt.

Contrary to popular opinion, wounds of the heart do not disappear with the passage of time. They may be buried in the memory bank somewhere. They may be repressed and locked away in the subconscious. Some people, due to wounds of the past, find themselves "acting out"—repeating the same behaviors they hated—creating in their family members the same wounds done to them. On the other side of the spectrum, there are those whose "acting out" because of wounds, rescues other people; these people's actions are praiseworthy in their eyes and in the eyes of others. There are people who by helping others somehow feel better within. Yet, the inner needs of the heart, which have rendered them diminished within, aren't addressed.

What we are really talking about here is people who have been sinned against by people they love and respect. The effects of these sins can be stuffed, and the memories altered to be something they weren't. The memories can be revised. But the bottom line is that we need to understand the concept of spiritual footholds of the enemy. Any area that we have not dealt with will be exposed by Satan's tempting and seducing spirits. The enemy will always seek to expand internal wounds to create inner strongholds of the heart that give us the message of hopelessness. That is his design to prevent our walking by faith in the peace and joy of the Holy Spirit. A stronghold of the heart and mind is any behavior or attitude in us we know to be contrary to the revealed will of God, and a sense of being without hope to change!

The Lord God operates in the eternal now, which pragmatically means that everything in life with which we have not adequately dealt, stands as an open offense against us before the Lord. The enemy knows where these wounds are and how to use them against us, to render us unable to walk in the precious provision of the grace of God.

When seeking to deal with these inner places of hopelessness created by having been sinned against, no amount of apology on our part for our feelings of hurt and wounding will help. Our own confession and repentance do not work on our wounds and inner heartaches because we aren't guilty of creating them. We don't need confession and repentance. We don't need to be forgiven. We need to be washed and healed inside by His precious provision. We need to be given mercy and forgiveness for our offenders— mercy and forgiveness we do not possess. We can then give to them, as He has given to us.

Please know the certainty of this one thing, children of God: The only way for people to be set free from sin of any type is for those issues of the heart and mind to be brought to the cross of Jesus Christ and crucified with Him there. There, at the cross of Jesus Christ our Lord, God does for us the remarkable spiritual transfer of the "unfair exchange." Jesus Christ our Lord became sin for us on the cross. All sin and its power to rule over us has been destroyed, even the sin done to me. By faith we come to His cross, bringing our wounds and heartaches to Jesus. We take the wounds out of our heart and lay them in His bosom. He takes them from us and destroys their power over us by crucifying them. Christ Jesus our Lord is the healing of God made available to us. As He healed people in the gospel records of His life, even so He heals His people's wounded hearts today. Listen deeply to these Scriptures that speak to this issue of the destruction of inner hopelessness because of sin done to us:

> God made him who had no sin to be sin for us, so that in him we might become the righteousness of God. (2 Cor. 5:21)

> And having disarmed the powers and authorities, he made a public spectacle of them, triumphing over them by the cross. (Col. 2:15)

> The weapons we fight with are not the weapons of the world. On the contrary, they have divine power to demolish strongholds. We demolish arguments and every pretension that sets itself up against the knowledge of God, and we take captive every thought and make it obedient to Christ. (2 Cor. 10:4–5)

Christ Jesus our Lord is the healing of God made available to us.

From a biblical and spiritual standpoint, there is just no question about it. The cross of Jesus Christ is the place where the power of God overcomes all of the power of the devil. It is in the precious shed blood of our Lord Jesus that all sin is completely washed from the human heart. That includes the sins done to us! It is at the cross of Jesus where God's powerful death blow was dealt to the power of sin to rule the human heart, mind, and memories with strongholds of hopelessness. It is the awesome truth of the risen and victorious King, Jesus Christ our Lord, living in the human heart by His Spirit that sets us free from the wounds and heartaches of the past.

The biblical truth to which I am seeking to direct our attention is our throne-room privileges as spiritual warriors of the faith. You and I have been given the right and the responsibility to choose the attitudes with which we will face life's circumstances. Thanks be unto Jesus, we can choose to attack the issues of our lives that have imprisoned us to fear or paralyzed us for years. In the provision of Christ Jesus, I am set free to choose the heart and attitude of an overcomer to face my inner giants of the heart one by one. In His provisions at the cross, I am given deep healing and forgiveness to extend to my offenders. As I take into my life His resurrection power, I am enabled to experience and live in His grace. Listen to the apostle Paul speak about these incredible provisions of the life of Jesus that are ours and are waiting to be taken by faith, regardless of the size of the inner issues:

> I keep asking that the God of our Lord Jesus Christ, the glorious Father, may give you the spirit of wisdom and revelation that you may know him better. I pray also that the eyes of your heart may be enlightened in order that you may know the hope to which he has called you, the riches of his glorious inheritance in the saints, and his incomparably great power for us who believe. That

> power is like the working of his mighty strength which
> he exerted in Christ when he raised him from the dead
> and seated him in the heavenly realms. (Eph. 1:17–20)

Here was a man who knew the tremendous pain of adversity—beatings, stonings, snakebite, imprisonments, and all kinds of persecutions—for his faith in Christ. Yet, in the midst of all of those incredible hardships, he wrote about the awesome power of God that is available to the children of God. In the context of a deepening, personal walk with the Lord Jesus by faith, there is the abundant storehouse of His provisions. We are given wisdom and revelation to know Him better. We are given eyes illuminated by His presence to see issues that have to be taken to the cross and destroyed. We are given His incomparably great resurrection power to live above sin, sin's power, the world's allure, and the inner, giant-sized issues created by wounds and heartaches of life.

In Christ Jesus my Lord and the choices His provision make available to me, I am able to choose the attitude that will rule my life. As I face and defeat internal, giant-sized issues one at time, He gives me His healing grace and mercy. I am set at peace with God, myself, and offenses of the past that have held me prisoner. I am set free more and more to walk with Him in His way for me. I am set free to see present adversities and adverse circumstances as cleverly disguised opportunities for me to learn what it means to honor, trust, and glorify my Master—no matter what comes my way. One of the constant themes of Scripture is the fact that, as God's sons and daughters, we are called to live above "just getting by." We are called to soar on wings like eagles, even though we may be presently surrounded by what appear to be turkeys or vultures!

Do you not know? Have you not heard? The Lord is the everlasting God, the Creator of the ends of the earth. He will not grow tired or weary, and his understanding no one can fathom. He gives strength to the weary and increases the power of the weak. Even youths grow tired and weary, and young men stumble and fall; but those who hope in the Lord will renew their strength. They will soar on wings like eagles; they will run and not grow weary, they will walk and not be faint. (Isa. 40:28–31)

In this book, I am going to encourage you repeatedly to make choices of your heart, to have the attitude of a God-honoring spiritual warrior as we face individual giants of the heart together. As we face and defeat them at the cross together, the attitude of an overcomer will, little by little, increase in measure within our hearts! Let's remember that the power to change is of God. He does the work in my heart as I appropriate His Word

> **. . . as God's sons and daughters, we are called to live above "just getting by."**

of truth. However, there are several things we need to possess as we approach this issue of the inner cleansing and healing of wounds of the heart. As we walk with Him in attacking the inner giants of the heart and mind, we need to embrace the following:

1. Choose to turn away from a mindset of hopelessness that says we cannot change something we know to be clearly against the will of God. His heart is for

me, and His role in my life is to transform me into the image of His Son Jesus. Brothers and sisters, that is definitely not a message of hopelessness to change. It is a clear call to be changed by God's powerful holy presence in our lives.

2. Choose the attitude of an overcomer to face the issues that have been defeating us from within. Because He has already won this internal victory of the heart, I can face the wounds and heartaches of the past with confidence born of faith in His revealed Word.

3. Choose a heart attitude—walking with the Spirit of the Lord—to meet with Jesus at the cross and there lay in Him what has been defeating us from within.

The warrior's heart needs healing, which the Lord Jesus Himself provides. Warriors are repaired and prepared to face life's giant-sized opponents of God, because they have been victorious over the giants within. I invite you to join me as we walk through these concepts of appropriating the provision of Jesus by faith, because we are taught to do so in the Word of God. I invite you to join me in walking with the Spirit of God to use His provisions in the painful, cruel, and difficult issues of our past and present.

Chapter Two

⚜

Six Biblical Overcomers as Giant-Slayers

L ET'S RESTATE THE OBVIOUS: Life is filled with hard places and difficulties. None of us is immune to personal heartache and pain. We often have no control over the circumstances and situations of life. The Lord Jesus said that the rain falls on the evil and on the good. Sometimes we make wrong choices, and the fruit of those choices are adversity and hardship. Sometimes we are victimized by the wrong choices of others, and we experience incredible pain through no fault of our own. While we can't choose our circumstances, we can and must choose to have a biblical attitude, a Christlike mindset, with which we will face life's wounds and hardships.

Permitting wounds or adversity to dictate our attitude is an enormous mistake. Some of my Christian brothers and sisters possess a negative attitude about life in general, and it is a huge handicap to place on ourselves. Beyond that, a negative attitude gives a place for the enemy to stand in our thinking. Some folks have chosen a what-can-go-wrong-will-go-wrong attitude, causing them to see what is wrong with everything and everybody and to see a problem in every opportunity. Problem dwelling or obstacle gazing can, and often does, lead to paralysis of our faith. It can cause God's people to view life's obstacles and hardships with the perspective of human resources and capabilities—or the lack thereof—and render us unable or unwilling to trust the Lord and walk with Him.

Some people are like the donkey, Ior, in the *Winnie-the-Pooh* stories. Ior's the guy who is always under his own personal rain cloud. When he talks, you feel like you have to help him finish his sentences. He has been utterly defeated by life, and his lack of vitality proves it. That is definitely not the life the Son of God bled and died to give to the sons and daughters of God. I have incredible difficulty in reconciling a defeatist attitude with biblical Christianity. Often defeatists believe so strongly that something bad is going to happen, that they fail to walk with God by faith. Instead of running into the arms of God by faith, these people turn away from Him and muddle through life, defeated and trying their best "to make it somehow."

The concept of being an overcomer for the kingdom of God is fleshed-out beautifully for me in the scriptural pictures of men and women who were heroes of the faith. In the Old Testament, there are portraits of men who trusted God and attacked giant-sized foes with faith. There were six men who went out for God, acted in faith, and overcame "giants" on the battlefield to the glory of God. Can you name them? Their names are Caleb (who attacked the giants at Hebron), David (who attacked Goliath of Gath), Abishai, Sibbecai, Elhanon, and Jonathan (David's nephew).

These men all understood the spiritual truth that our heart attitudes—the way we choose to live our lives—are choices of the heart. They chose to face the giants, opposing them with deep trust and surrender to the will of God. They had three things in common:

1. They all possessed great faith in God's ability to provide for them and care for them. They talked about winning before they even went out to fight!
2. They all possessed enormous amounts of courage, because they were convinced of the majesty and magnitude of God.
3. They chose an optimistic attitude, which saw the possibilities for the glory of God, while facing undefeatable giants bellowing at them, "You can't beat me!"

Biblical Overcomer Caleb

Caleb's life is an absolute miracle. The man was eighty-five years old, a man of God who had weathered forty years in the wilderness because ten of his fellow spies gave a negative and defeatist report about the Promised Land. Yet, as we read about his life in Joshua 14, he is an eighty-five-year-old wiry guy who is ready to take on the most difficult of the people who lived in the Promised Land. He came to Joshua with a request for his own inheritance to be granted to him according to the word of Moses. He had fought for everyone else, now he wanted to fight for his own family's heritage.

Now give me this hill country that the Lord promised me that day. You yourself heard that the Anakites were there and their cities were large and fortified, but, the Lord helping me I will drive them out. (Josh. 14:12)

I love it! The guy is eighty-five and testifying with wonderful words of faith about God's goodness and provision. "I am just as tough as I was when I was forty years old, Joshua. Give me the giant-occupied hill country around Hebron. The Lord and my family and I will drive them out!" I have decided I want to be like Caleb when I grow up. When I am eighty-five, I want to be a man of deepening trust and relational love with the Lord, a man who is concerned about the advance of God's Kingdom in my own heart, in churches, and through His people!

Biblical Overcomer David

Our second giant-slayer was a young shepherd boy named David. He was sent by his father, Jesse, with provisions of food for his older brothers, who were in King Saul's army. They were on the battlefront, preparing for war with the Philistines. As we enter the scene of 1 Samuel 17, it is not a pretty picture. Israel's army is cowering in fear, as every day for forty days, the gigantic killing machine, Goliath of Gath, comes out and defies them to send out a man to do *mano-y-mano* battle to the death. Goliath shouts in defiance at the Lord Jehovah and His army.

Day after day, Israel's army sits at their battle lines, paralyzed by fear while "serving the Lord of Hosts." What's wrong with this picture? The nine-foot-six-inch giant is opposing God, reviling Him, and there isn't a soldier in His army who seems to believe God will aid him to silence this defilement.

David comes to the camp to give his brothers their food and to take back news to his dad about them. As the shepherd boy carries out his task, he witnesses Goliath coming out and shouting his usual defiance and defiling the atmosphere with his daily challenge and obscenities.

I love 1 Samuel 17:23*b*; It says that Goliath was ". . . shouting his usual defiance, and *David heard it*" (emphasis mine). David's heart of love for God is stirred. He is moved to faith, grief, and anger all at once. He asks permission of King Saul to go out to meet Goliath. Having obtained the king's blessing, he chooses five smooth stones, takes his shepherd's sling, and goes out to meet the giant problem.

As David goes out, fear gives way to faith, courage, and optimism. The boy is secure in his heart that God is going to deliver him—just as God had helped him prevail over the lions and bears he'd encountered while tending his father's sheep. Look at this teenage giant-slayer's words with me, and feel his heart of faith swell with God's anointing:

> You come against me with sword, spear and javelin, but I come against you in the Name of the Lord Almighty. . . . This day the Lord will hand you over to me and I'll strike you down. . . . All those gathered here will know that it is not by sword or spear that the Lord saves; for the battle is the Lord's and he will give you into our hands. (1 Sam. 17:45–47)

David had eyes to see what no other man could see. The Lord had already provided the victory over the giant. It just had to be believed and claimed by faith. In my mind's eye, there were two twelve-foot-tall angels standing behind Goliath, God's giant-sized enemy. One angel held a target above Goliath's head that said, "Hit him here, Davey!" The other angel was holding a projectile funnel with a wide opening and the constricted end right in front of Goliath's forehead. As David went out he ran toward him. This kid had a can't-miss mentality! You know the story well. David made Goliath considerably shorter than his nine-foot-six-inch frame had been before the battle. The giant-sized problem was history!

Biblical Overcomers Abishai, Sibbecai, Elhanon, and Jonathan

Because David was a giant-slayer, he attracted other men of valor, who became men of faith, courage, and optimism and who slew giants. David had four men in his army who were giant-slayers for God. They, like their commander David, had attacked and killed giant-sized killing machines who stood in opposition to the armies of God.

The spiritual principle is this: *We reproduce what we are in the lives of others in our sphere of influence!* People of faith, courage, and optimism inspire others to be people of faith as well. It was true of a shepherd boy, whom God called and made a king. It is still true today in the family of faith. When we attack and defeat giant-sized problems in our lives, we inspire an atmosphere of faith for others in our church families!

In following chapters, we are going to look at giants of the heart and mind that we need to face. Our word-picture for attacking these giants will be those six men we studied, so we might learn from their inspiring models of faith and victory!

I'm convinced God wants to inspire us to meet life's demands from the perspective of Jesus' victory and provision for us. When we choose to face life with faith and confidence in who He is and what He has said He will do, we have embarked on an adventure. He will lead us to an attitude of courage and confidence in His victory in the face of life's giants. I am totally convinced this is what life is all about. We are here to learn to walk by faith with our awe-inspiring, omnipotent God who delights in His children. He has so much more spiritual victory for us than we understand, let alone than we have yet appropriated by faith.

Genuine faith is taking God at His word and living like we believe it's true! God delights in us so much. He longs for us to know Him more intimately, and provides spiritual riches for us in Christ. He wants to walk with us and reveal His glory on the earth. He delights in simple, childlike, trusting prayer, offered in faith and based on His promises. Some people look at David's

> **When we attack and defeat giant-sized problems in our lives, we inspire an atmosphere of faith for others . . .**

attack on Goliath as the boy putting himself on the line that day. My perspective is that he put God on the line that day. Do we think God was afraid of a pip-squeak, nine-foot-tall human being?

Here's the bottom line, giant-slayers: In the same way eighty-five-year-old men and teenage boys don't attack giant-sized killing machines in their own strength and win, you and I do not win spiritual victories over life's unconquerable foes in our own strength. When there seems to be no way, we need the Lord Jesus to come to us and make a way for us. Giant-slayers earnestly desire the glory of God to be made manifest in their lives and through their circumstances on the earth.

I can do everything through him who gives me strength.
(Phil. 4:13)

But we have this treasure in jars of clay to show that the
all-surpassing power is from God and not from us.
(2 Cor. 4:7)

Giant-slayers understand that the outcome of their
struggles and hard places in life are not dependent on their
resources or lack thereof. Life's giants are faced and defeated by taking the Lord at His Word and by boldly proclaiming His provisions for us! We trust in His mighty power. God wants to use us and our circumstances as instruments of His glory on the earth. The sooner we learn that, the better, so we can get on with the battle. God is looking for people who are wholly His, trusting Him regardless of circumstances.

> **Genuine faith is taking God at His word and living like we believe it's true!**

For the eyes of the Lord range throughout the earth to
strengthen those whose hearts are fully devoted to him.
(1 Chron. 16:9b)

Stick with me, and let's walk through this study of what
present-day giant-slayers look like—those who choose to
go into His battles while taking and proclaiming His Word
and His provisions of victory. If we are people who please
God and walk in spiritual victory, it is because we have

decided to trust the Lord to give us His life and resurrection power each day. His eyes are ranging over the earth, looking for those who trust Him, who are convinced of their own weakness but also are convinced of His love and power. He strongly supports those who believe and long for His glory on the earth!

Chapter Three

The Five Smooth Stones Today's Giant-Slayers Need

O N HIS WAY OUT for his encounter with Goliath, David needed some weapons. He stopped at a nearby brook and selected five smooth stones to throw at the giant who stood in the valley shouting, "You can't beat me!" David planned to use these stones as projectiles from his shepherd's sling. He planned to have maximum impact on the forehead of the giant-sized obstacle standing before him.

In this chapter, we begin our consideration of how our Lord God wants us to be overcomers of the inner giants of the heart. Using the analogy of David's five smooth stones, we will look at the provisions the Lord Jesus has made available to us. What Jesus did for us on the cross, overcame all of the power of the enemy.

The reason the Son of God appeared was to destroy the devil's work. (1 John 3:8*b*)

Our personal response of faith in Christ Jesus destroys every scheme and tactic and weapon the enemy uses to keep us in prisons of the heart. Listen to these wonderful words from Psalm 107:10–16, regarding God's desire to set us free from these inner prisons:

> Some sat in darkness and the deepest gloom, prisoners suffering in iron chains, for they had rebelled against the words of God and despised the counsel of the Most High. So he subjected them to bitter labor; they stumbled, and there was no one to help. Then they cried to the Lord in their trouble, and he saved them from their distress. He brought them out of darkness and the deepest gloom and broke away their chains. Let them give thanks to the Lord for his unfailing love and his wonderful deeds to men, for he breaks down gates of bronze and cuts through bars of iron.

The Sling of Faith

Using the analogy of David's weapons, I want us to think about the weapons God's people use to attack the giants of the heart. I want to start by saying that I believe the Lord's wonderful gift of faith is analogous to David's shepherd's sling. It is the instrument David used to propel the smooth stones. Faith is the instrument God's sons and daughters use to propel our smooth stones at our inner giants. By faith, we are able to apprehend and are apprehended by the Word of God, and by faith we lay hold of His promises made to us in His Word!

The faith to believe the Lord is a gift of God's Holy Spirit, making it possible for us to take Him at His Word and live like we believe it is true. Faith considers Him faithful to His promises, because He has authored and pioneered the way of faith for us. Faith believes that He is who He says He is, and that He does what He says He will do. Faith prays into existence God's revealed desire, regardless of evidence to the contrary. Faith first resided in God's heart before it was expressed to us. He first believed that if He gave His Son Jesus as Lord and Savior and as sin offering to redeem us, we would respond to that gift, turn from our sins, and trust His provision for our salvation. God first demonstrated faith, then gave us the gift of faith so we could respond to His drawing love.

> ### . . . by faith we lay hold of His promises made to us in His Word!

As we take this gift of faith He offers and believe Him to save us, the Word of God springs to life, and a relationship with our Creator begins. He takes us deeper into faith in the same way that He initiated us into our walk of faith with Him. We don't develop faith as though it were some physical muscle or something we can work up on our own. Quite to the contrary, faith is always and forever the gift of God. Paul tells us we deepen our faith when we believe the Word of God and choose to take His promises personally. Romans 10:17 says,

> Faith comes by hearing the message and hearing the message comes by the Word of God.

Faith (an action word) actively operates in correlation with the desire of God's heart as revealed through the Word of Christ. By believing God regardless of circumstances or evidence that seems contrary, a new reality, or dimension, of faith with God is created for us. Faith believes that ultimate reality is what God says He is doing or is going to do. Paul wrote a tremendous word about this is 2 Corinthians 4:16–18:

> Therefore we do not lose heart. Though outwardly we are wasting away, yet inwardly we are being renewed day by day. For our light and momentary troubles are achieving for us an eternal glory that far outweighs them all. So we fix our eyes not on what is seen, but on what is unseen. For what is seen is temporary, but what is unseen is eternal.

> **By believing God regardless of circumstances or evidence that seems contrary, a new reality, or dimension, of faith with God is created for us.**

The outstanding example of faith in Scripture is Abraham. He is referred to as the father of all who have believed God's perspective of reality is what really matters. He is the father of all who believe and aggressively take hold of God's provisions by faith. Paul spoke of Abraham's outstanding faith by telling us three things he believed about God, which enabled him to obtain life and godliness from the Lord. All three of these things Abraham believed, and it was credited

to him as righteousness. We read about them in the text of
Romans 4:17–22:

1. Abraham believed that God gives life to the dead.
   His ability to procreate with his wife, Sarah, in order to have the child of promise was, in fact, dead.
   As a matter of reality check for us as rational people,
   Sarah never could have children!
2. Abraham believed that God calls things that are not
   yet as though they already physically exist. How often we read God speaking prophetically—through
   the Old Testament prophets—a word that is pertains
   to some future event, and yet it is written in the
   past tense. It already had been done in God's heart!
3. Abraham believed God has the power to do what
   He has said He will do. Paul told the Corinthians
   that the promises of God are all "Yes" in Christ, and
   through us believing them and confessing them into
   existence in prayer, we pronounce the "amen."
   Abraham acted in faith and conceived a son in his
   ninety-plus-year-old wife's barren womb!

Getting back to the analogy. Faith is analogous to David's
sling, which he used to propel the smooth stone toward
Goliath's forehead. Faith operates in our lives by our choice.
It is the gift of God, but it is the prerogative of the children
of God to put into action. The Lord delights to have His
Word received and believed in the recreated human spirit
and then confessed through lips of faith. When we bring
His promises to our minds and pray them back to Him, He
doesn't wring His hands and wish He hadn't made such an
outlandish offer! He has the power to do what He has said

He will do, so let's believe Him and confess His promises as true. When it comes to confessing His Word in faith, any lips of faith will do! He delights to work in concert with His people who invite Him to do so.

Having discussed the shepherd's sling that propels the five smooth stones into action, I want to look at the five weapons we have available to us as God's children to attack the inner giants of the heart. Let's consider them together.

Smooth Stone #1: The Living Word of God

When choosing to attack the inner giants of the heart, the child of God must be well armed. The most important smooth stone to carry in your shepherd's bag is the one you throw first, the Word of God. The Word is a weapon, when confessed with faith and surrender. Paul told the Ephesian believers they needed to take unto themselves the weapon of "the sword of the Spirit which is the Word of God" as part of their armor. The author of the Book of Hebrews wrote a really marvelous passage of Scripture regarding the powerful, active nature of the Word of the Lord:

> For the Word of God is living and active. Sharper than any double-edged sword, it penetrates even to dividing soul and spirit, joints and marrow; it judges the thoughts and attitudes of the heart. Nothing in all creation is hidden from God's sight. Everything is uncovered and laid bare before the eyes of him to whom we must give account. (4:12–13)

What the Lord wants us to understand regarding this scripture is the profound, dividing effect the Word of God has upon me as I receive it and believe it. It literally divides between where my soul has been wounded, where hurts and heartaches live in me, and where my recreated spirit wants to soar with the Holy Spirit. The Lord will take me to words of Scripture that will, under His counsel, lay bare things in my soul that are open sores of the heart, perhaps deeply repressed memories. Things, such as old wounds I may have forgotten about but that remain in my subconscious mind, will be brought out into the light as I walk by faith with the Light of the World. He will reveal the discrepancy between the place of my wounded soul and where my recreated spirit longs to do great exploits of faith with the Holy Spirit.

The truth of this should be obvious to even the casual observer, let alone to the person who would attack the inner giants of the heart. If there are old wounds, hurts, or heartaches that are in us and we don't know about them, or they're deeply buried in our memory, we'll never be able to defeat them. What we can't see we can't attack. That's precisely why we need to hear the fresh and powerful word of God preached and taught. The Word is living and active; the word used in the text is *rhema*, a living sword of the Spirit.

We sometimes need to be shown by God what is really in our hearts, as well as what the Spirit would like us to do about what we see there. As long as the memories or hurts stay in the darkness, the inner giants of the heart are free to bellow at us, "You can't beat me!" In essence it is true because you can't beat what you can't see. The wonderful author of the Word lives in our hearts. Jesus called Him "another Counselor" sent to be with us and live in our hearts. The Word is our first smooth stone that we are to throw at the inner giants. It is a weapon we depend on the Lord to give us as we cooperate with Him.

A number of years ago the US military came up with new weaponry that had computer guidance systems that greatly increased accuracy for bombing specific targets many miles away. They appropriately named these weapons "smart bombs." During the Gulf War many people saw the picture of one of these bombs entering into the chimney of a building and totally leveling it. (The thought crossed my mind about the number of people that may have been in that building—people whose eternal destiny was just settled for them.) However, what I want to draw from that picture is the fact that the Word of God is powerful and effective. When believed and confessed in faith against the internal giants of the heart, God's Word, like a computer guided missile, strikes with deadly accuracy, exploding the myths and lies the giant bellows at us from within!

For the remainder of the smooth stones as the weaponry of God, I turn your attention to James 4:6–10. The Lord has given His sons and daughters some awesome miracles of the heart through appropriating by faith the weapons of the Spirit found in this passage. Let's look at them together.

Smooth Stone #2: Brokenness of Heart

James writes some tremendous words to us about our need of more grace from the Lord. Essentially the inner giants of the heart live in areas where we have taken our own human ways and have not experienced His powerful provisions of grace and mercy, His deep forgiveness in our lives. He tells us there is abundant grace for the humble, brokenhearted person. However, God opposes the proud person who thinks he or she can make it on their own. The

Book of James tells us in chapter 4, verse 6, to be embracing a deep, humble, contrite and broken heart before God:

> But he gives us more grace. That is why Scripture says: God opposes the proud but gives grace to the humble.

Brokenness as an inner attitude of the heart is cherished by God the Father, Son, and Lord Spirit. It is an atmosphere of the heart in which He delights to work. However, in our culture in North America, we cherish our rugged individualism. We feel confident we can pull ourselves up by our own bootstraps. Give us the latest self-help book on the market, show us how to "do it yourself" and fix it quickly, and then get out of our way. We espouse this and then wonder why we are such a society of the lonely and why hopelessness is the spirit of the age. We keep telling ourselves and acting as if we don't need anybody for anything, and we exclude everyone from helping us, including God.

... the Word of God is powerful and effective. ... [it] strikes with deadly accuracy, exploding the myths and lies the giant bellows at us from within!

The proud person keeps saying, "I can do this. I don't need anybody." The humble person bows before the throne of grace and cries out to God for mercy from a broken heart.

"Lord God, I can't make it without you, and I am tired of trying to make it on my own. Please come and minister to me." The Psalmist David wrote in Psalm 51:17:

> The sacrifices of God are a broken spirit; a broken and contrite heart, O God, you will not despise.

The inner giants of the heart hate humility and brokenness in the children of God. They understand what can and usually does happen when the child of God is broken in heart: generally, he or she reaches for the other three stones in the brook.

Stone #3: Confession of Our Need

James goes on to explain to us our next smooth-stone weapon in verse seven of the passage when he tells the children of God:

> Submit yourselves, then, to God. Resist the devil and he will flee from you.

When we are broken in heart before the Lord, it is the next logical step to move on to confess our need to God. We will invariably open up to Him, confessing our need and our desire to have Him move in our lives to meet our needs. When we confess our needs at the throne of God, crying out to Him for mercy, we are submitting ourselves to God. Further, such ones are in reality, resisting the devil's workings.

Satan is the "prince of darkness." He dwells in and is enabled to work in our hearts— sometimes unhindered and perhaps even undetected—when we keep hidden, by choice or blindness, hurts and heartaches from our past. When we are unwilling or unable to bring things out into the open, the enemy stands in them as entry points, or footholds, and ultimately strongholds of inner hopelessness. When these issues are brought out into the open by confessing them to the Light of the World, Jesus, they are in the light, and the darkness immediately loses power.

The smooth stone of confession of our needs (with the concomitant confession of the Word of God to meet our needs) is a powerful weapon in the shepherd's sling of faith. The inner giants of the heart crumble when we remove their right to stand in the entry points of wounding or heartaches of the past. When we bring these to our gracious King Jesus and He pours us full of mercy and forgiveness by His Spirit, there is cleansing and healing grace flowing through us, remitting the sins done to us. We are literally handed forgiveness to extend to our offender, something we could never do for ourselves!

Smooth Stone #4: Coming Near to Him at the Cross

James goes on to the fourth smooth stone the child of God needs as a weapon to propel at the inner giants of the heart. He says in verse 8*a*, "Come near to God." The child of God is invited to draw near to God by faith—to enter into the provisions Jesus Christ our Lord has made available to us on the cross by the working of His Spirit in us.

One of the things that we have to receive by faith, certainly not by reason, is that the Lord God is eternal, and He operates beyond space and time. What that means to us pragmatically is that everything is "in the now" to God. One of the things that operates in the eternal now in the heart of God is the cross on which our Lord Jesus gave Himself as the redemption price the Father required to set us free from sins and iniquities. He gave Himself for us to wash away all sins, including the ones done to us. We can walk by faith, with the Holy Spirit, to the cross and meet with Jesus there any time.

We can draw near to Him at the cross by faith and lay things, such as wounds—those painful memories of sins done to us that the enemy has used as entry points or footholds against us—in His bosom. He will take them from us, bear them away from us, and release us from sins of our own doing as well as those done against us. As we do this, what oppressed us and imprisoned us is crucified with Him. The power of the inner giants of the heart is destroyed in Christ Jesus. What the Son of God crucifies on our behalf is destroyed for all who believe!

> **We can walk by faith, with the Holy Spirit, to the cross and meet with Jesus there any time.**

Smooth Stone #5: The Filling of the Holy Spirit

James shows the children of God the fifth smooth stone we can use as a weapon against the inner giants of the heart. He tells us that when we draw near to God, He will draw near to us. Brokenness, confession, drawing near to God at the cross of Jesus, and laying in Him things that have imprisoned us are all good and cathartic things to do. But the fact of the matter is, we desperately need to be renewed and empowered by the Holy Spirit of God. We need Him to

live in us in power in the very places where we have confessed and invited Jesus to crucify what stood against us.
The child of God always has the joy of knowing that
the Father's heart of love for us moves Him to fill us with
His Spirit when we ask. He wants very much to walk with
us in the garden of our soul. He wants to know us and to be
known by us. It is the promise of Jesus our Lord that He
will send us the Comforter to dwell in us. It is the awesome
privilege of every child of God to go on being filled with
the Holy Spirit every day (see Eph. 5:17–18).

When we have had the Lord Jesus bear away from us
issues of the past that have imprisoned us, the enemy's beings will not give up easily. The darkness doesn't surrender
territory without a fight. We need the Lord Jesus Himself
standing up in us powerfully against the reinvasion of the
darkness that will attempt to reclaim territory of old sinful
patterns, wounds, hurts, or heartaches that were once points
of entry into our thinking. Jesus told His disciples that evil
spirits will try to reoccupy what they have once had. If the
house is merely swept and put in order but not filled with
the power and life of the Lord, there will be ruin in that
house. The bottom line is, we are no match for the evil
one's capabilities. We are, however, in Christ Jesus our Lord,
more than conquerors!

Well, there you have the five smooth stones that every
child of God needs to propel by faith at the inner giants of
the heart. As these giants shout, "You can't beat me! You
can't get rid of me that easily!" their message is one of hopelessness. But we can confidently answer their tyrannical rages
this way: "That's right, I can't beat you. But I have met Jesus
Christ my Lord, and He tells me in His Word that He has
defeated all of the works of sin and death and all the powers

of hell at the cross. And if you stick with me for just a little while longer, I'm going to walk by faith and meet with my Savior who defeated your lord. He will deal with you!"

Perhaps you are wondering why you and I need to throw five stones at the giants of the heart and David only had to throw one stone. It is really quite simple. David was an exceptionally good shot! How many times have you or I used a sling and smooth stones anyway?

You have read this far with me. Stick with me, and let's go throw some stones together!

Part Two

Giants of the Heart Imposed on Us by the Enemy

Chapter Four

Defeating the Giant of Temptation

THE LORD GOD DELIGHTS in being trusted by His children. He reveals Himself in Scripture as a strong tower and a mighty fortress—a faithful Lord who desires to cover and protect His sons and daughters. He delights in our choosing to have an attitude of faith regardless of our circumstances. Listen to two passages of Scripture, from the Psalms, that are just precious to the heart of the child of God:

> I love you, O Lord my strength. The Lord is my rock, my fortress and my deliverer, my God is my rock in whom I take refuge. He is my shield and the horn of my salvation, my stronghold. I call to the Lord, who is worthy of praise, and I am saved from my enemies. (18:1–3)

> "Because he loves me," says the Lord, "I will rescue him; I will protect him, for he acknowledges my name. He will call upon me, and I will answer him; I will be with

him in trouble, I will deliver him and honor him. With long life will I satisfy him and show him my salvation." (91:14–16)

One of my life verses, which the Lord gave me early in my Christian walk, is found in 2 Chronicles 16:9b: "The eyes of the Lord range throughout the earth to strengthen those whose hearts are fully committed to him." What this verse says to the person with eyes of faith and a heart to receive from the Lord is that God is interested in watching over us, empowering us to walk with Him, and enabling us work with Him in the world.

Armed with the knowledge that God cares about us and watches over us with jealous love, let's attack and defeat our first enemy-imposed giant of the heart: *temptation.*

In referring to temptation as a giant of the heart, imposed upon us by the enemy, I am speaking to the issue of how it begins and gains entry into us. Satan is the author of temptation, seducing, and enticing Christians to enter in to some form of sinful behavior. It begins with an external stimulus aimed at the unrighteous satisfaction of one of the appetites of our humanity. It seeks to entice the person being tempted to dwell on the stimulus until it has entered into the person's thought processes. When it has gained entry into the thoughts and has been considered in the heart, temptation entices our desires and ultimately we choose to reject the loving ways of God. The choice is made to turn away from the holy ways of God the Holy Spirit and to embrace satisfying a human appetite in some sinful manner. Consider with me some foundational truths regarding this inner giant of temptation that stands in the human heart on a daily basis, shouting, "You can't beat me!"

1. The act of being tempted is common to every person who has ever or will ever live. Christians, far from being immune to temptation, are very often the special targets of the enemy Satan's more ingenious temptations. We are God's sons and daughters. As such, we are marked out for special hatred by Satan, who absolutely detests righteousness on the earth, especially in believers.

2. Temptation to sin is not synonymous with having sinned. Temptation doesn't mean we are forsaken by God, nor does it mean there is something inherently evil about us. God often uses the enemy's tempting works as an opportunity to show us something about ourselves that He wants to change. But that doesn't mean necessarily that we have sinned. We don't defeat temptation by repentance of it, but by rejecting it and turning away from it. Dwelling on it, mulling it over, and actually choosing the wrong is sinful, and it is our sin that requires our repentance.

3. Even our Lord and Savior Jesus was, under the Holy Spirit's guidance, led into the wilderness to be tempted by the evil one. Yet Scripture clearly shows us He was without sin.

Then Jesus was led by the Spirit into the desert to be tempted by the devil. (Matt. 4:1)

For we do not have a high priest who is unable to sympathize with our weaknesses, but we have one who has been tempted in every way, just as we are, yet was without sin. Let us then approach the throne of grace with confidence, so that we may receive mercy and find grace to help us in our time of need. (Heb. 4:15–16)

4. We are not tempted because we are sinful, we are tempted because we are human. As human beings, we are involved in a cosmic struggle for the souls and the worshipful allegiance of all of "the peoples." The enemy seeks to steal the glory of God from human lips. He does this by enticing human beings to sinful behavior—behavior that offends our Father God's holy nature, placing a dividing wall between God and us.

5. Jesus Christ our Lord became a human being and was tempted, in every way just as we are. He defeated Satan's tempting works and then went to the cross and destroyed all of the enemy's power over us in sin and sin's penalty of death. For all of us who believe in Him and receive His grace by faith, we are given victory over the enemy and his temptation as spiritual overcomers in Christ Jesus. God has made a way for us to deal with and defeat temptation. His Name is Jesus Christ our Lord.

No temptation has seized you except what is common to man. And God is faithful: He will not let you be tempted beyond what you can bear. But when you are tempted, he will also provide a way out so that you can stand up under it. (1 Cor. 10:13)

Temptation in Our Lives

The first thing I'd like us to understand about temptation is its nature and purpose; we can do so by looking at the nature and purpose of its author. Let's first be clear about the fact that God doesn't tempt us. That is the work of the enemy Satan and his beings.

Blessed is the man who perseveres under trial, because when he has stood the test, he will receive the crown of life that God has promised to those who love him. When tempted, no one should say, "God is tempting me." For God cannot be tempted by evil, nor does he tempt anyone. (James 1:12–13)

When we walk in difficult seasons of temptation, we are not forsaken by God. You and I are loved by Him. The fact of this scripture verse is that God sets the limit of the temptation. He uses the enemy's enticements in us as a refining act. He is concerned that we will be more in love with Him than we ever were before. He permits us to be tempted and enticed so that we may learn more of His loving grace and spiritual provisions for us in Christ Jesus.

> **We are not tempted because we are sinful, we are tempted because we are human.**

Notice with me these incredible words about the devil's nature and purpose in Matthew 4:1–3a:

> Then Jesus was led by the Spirit into the desert to be tempted by the devil. After forty days and forty nights he was hungry. Then the tempter came to him.

Temptation is permitted by God but is authored by the enemy. Satan hates our God and opposes the Lord's authority, rulership and glory. The devil's nature is to rebel against God, and his purpose is to lead an active rebellion against the will of God that is being carried out on the earth. Scripturally speaking, temptation is enticement by the evil one's kingdom beings to get us to choose not to obey God or to love good and do right.

Temptations offer the lure of following after self-will and human desires rather than submitting to God's rulership. And all the while, as we think we're doing our own thing, we are being led by a huge spiritual nose ring into the enemy's scheming plan to revolt against the Lord God. It is a subtle and progressive scheming tactic, through the establishment of sin and guilt in our lives, to ultimately steal our hearts and minds away from glorifying God. The goal is to get us to break our fellowship with the Lord by taking our own way. Unfortunately, and often too late, we learn that this is the way of sin and it is actually Satan's way for us.

Temptation in us will always be fought on at least one of the following three specific battlefronts: (1) the flesh; (2) the world; and (3) the footholds where the enemy can stand in us. I want us to see how the Lord Jesus was tempted in all three of these places and note that He used the Word of God—God's revealed will—to defeat the enemy at each place.

First, the human appetites we all have are a part of our humanity. These are created by God and are in themselves good; yet when they are perverted by the sinful nature, they can absolutely rule over us. Appetites for food, sexual expression, play, success, and so on are great, but perverted under the rule of the sinful nature, these can consume us. The enemy tempted Jesus in His human appetite for food after He had fasted for forty days. In Matthew 4:3 the enemy enticed Him to command the stones to be made into bread. Jesus replied from the Word of God, "It is written, man does not live by bread alone, but on every word that comes from the mouth of God" (Matt. 4:4).

Second, the worldly system of values stands in direct opposition to all that is holy and righteous in the sight of God. The worldly system is a combination of the sinful ways of people and the wiles of the enemy Satan. The enemy's goal in using the worldly system as a temptation point is to have us follow sinful expressions of our appetites. The enemy tempted the Lord Jesus to go to the very pinnacle of the temple and throw Himself down in front of all of the onlooking worshipers at Jerusalem. Satan enticed Jesus to use His God-given spiritual power to let all the world know how magnificent He really is and to prove that He really is the Son of God. Then to enhance the temptation, Satan even misquoted a scripture regarding angelic protection. Jesus passed by the temptation to worldly acclaim when He quoted the scripture, "It is written: Do not put the Lord your God to the test" (Matt. 4:7).

Third, the enemy seeks to establish footholds in our hearts by leading us to sins of commission or of omission. The enemy will seek to use against us anything we haven't owned, confessed, and of which we have not repented. Unconfessed sins, like a willful misuse of God's grace and mercy, stand in us as places in our hearts that are not washed by the blood of Jesus. These are legal footholds that the enemy targets for his work in our lives. The enemy tempted Jesus, promising that if Jesus would worship him, he would, in fact, give Jesus all the kingdoms and splendor of the world. Jesus saw through the enemy's enticement as a place for the enemy to gain a foothold in His life. He defeated the enemy by quoting the scripture, "Away from me Satan! It is written, 'Worship the Lord your God, and serve Him only'" (Matt. 4:10).

There is a place in the Hudson River where, as you sail along, you seem hemmed in by the hills. The boat sails forward toward a rocky wall, and it seems as if it must either stop or be dashed to pieces. Just as you come within the shadow of the mountain, an opening suddenly appears. The boat passes through the opening into one of the grandest bays in the river. So it is with temptations of the enemy. We ought not to seek it or enter into it; God promises no way out if we do. But if it meets us on our journey to heaven, we go straight toward the heart of God. His way out will reveal itself in time; if we will only stay on our journey, God will make a way out so we can bear up under it.

The Temptation of Joseph

In Genesis 39, there is a story of the young man named Joseph who had been sold into slavery in Egypt by his brothers, who were jealous of him. He wanted desperately to be a man of God. He lived by the principles of honesty and integrity he had learned in his father's home. He knew he must follow God's ways to live under His blessing.

The story goes that a man named Potiphar bought Joseph on the slave block and took him home. Everything to which Joseph put his hand for his master, Potiphar, prospered and was blessed by God. The Egyptian soon noticed this and put his whole house under Joseph's direction. The man's wife had physical designs on the handsome, young Hebrew slave and enticed him again and again to come to bed with her. Each time he spurned her advances, explaining to her that he had to honor both God and Potiphar. He wouldn't disgrace his earthly master by sleeping with his wife.

This woman's desires, however seemed to be out of control. She wouldn't relent and kept up the pursuit day after day. She finally caught Joseph in a predicament where he was alone with her and she had hold of his outer garment. He was so urgent to get away from her that he slipped out of his garment and ran out of the room. Then she turned the tables on him. She told her husband he had tried to rape her and had fled, leaving behind his garment. Her husband was enraged and had Joseph thrown in prison for a crime he didn't commit.

> **We don't have to surrender one inch of ground to the enemy when he attacks us with temptations.**

The thing we need to see here is, through all of these events of false accusation and slander, even to the point of spending several years in prison, this young man stayed true to the Lord and lived by his convictions. He turned away from temptation and stayed pure. Joseph, like Jesus who lived hundreds of years later, showed us the truth that we don't have to cave in to the temptations the enemy throws at us. We can turn away from them and choose to stay clean before God.

We are taught about the spiritual warfare by Paul in the letter to the Ephesians. In chapter 6, verses 10 and following, he compares our life—our physical, mental, emotional, and spiritual body—to "ground." He tells the Ephesians, and all of us, that we are responsible to stand our ground against the enemy's schemes and wiles. We don't have to surrender one inch of ground to the enemy when he attacks us with temptations. This inner, enemy-imposed giant of the heart can be faced and defeated by the child of God in the mighty name of Jesus. We have the whole armor of God available to us, giant-slayers. So let's go over to the brook on the way to the battle. Let's pick out some smooth stones and go after this giant of temptation with faith and courage, knowing full well that the battle is the Lord's!

Smooth Stone #1: The Word of God

Please notice with me that when the Lord Jesus faced the tempting and enticing of Satan himself, the weapon the Lord used against the prince of darkness was the Word of God. He knew the Word of God, and He confessed the Word of God as a spiritual military act of faith. Three times the enemy enticed Jesus, and three times Jesus said, "It is written." Jesus did this the exact same way you and I can do. He was filled with and was led by the Holy Spirit. Matthew 4:1 says, "Jesus was led by the Spirit into the desert to be tempted by the devil."

It is the Holy Spirit's role to make the Word of God a consuming fire in our hearts and a weapon against the enemy when it is confessed through our lips. The first battlefield the Spirit leads us to conquer is our own heart's propensity to fall for the tempting and enticing of the enemy. Before we are ready to face and defeat other giants, we have to face and defeat the temptation to choose a path of sin. In the heat of temptations from the darkness, children of God, we can rest on the words of the Lord Jesus regarding the role of the Counselor. The Holy Spirit's role to is bring to our remembrance everything He has taught us:

> If anyone loves me, he will obey my teaching. My Father will love him and we will come to him and make

our home with him. He who does not love me will not obey my teaching. These words you hear are not my own; they belong to the Father who sent me. All this I have spoken while still with you. But the Counselor, the Holy Spirit, whom the Father will send in my name, will teach you all things and will remind you of everything I have said to you" (John 14:23-26).

Smooth Stone #2: Brokenness of Heart

Knowing the love God has for us, we can allow the Lord to use the enemy's temptations and enticements to show us things in our own lives that are displeasing to God. Repeated assaults at us by the evil one's tempters, in any given area of our lives, are a message to the spiritually discerning child of God. There is an area of weakness that needs to be dealt with or the enemy wouldn't keep aiming at it. Temptation can be a schoolmaster to point us to our need of more grace in

> **Temptation can be a schoolmaster to point us to our need of more grace in an area of our lives . . .**

an area of our lives where we are presently vulnerable. We can embrace a broken and contrite heart when we see desires in our hearts that are definitely dishonoring to God. We can choose to own those feelings within, knowing the Word of God teaches us that He delights in the sacrifices of a broken and contrite heart.

Smooth Stone #3: Confession of Our Need

Offering the Lord Jesus my brokenness of heart and confessing the need I see, is definitely God's road to spiritual power and authority in the battlefield of the human heart. When, as a result of the enemy's temptations in a given area, I confess my need in that area of my life, there is profound joy in God's heart. He delights in His children who will spurn the ways of human provisions for ourselves. He loves to hear the deep cry of our hearts as we confess our need of His provisions for us.

Smooth Stone #4: Drawing Near to Jesus at the Cross

When we pour out our brokenhearted confession to the Lord Jesus by faith at the cross, there is a flow of God's powerful spiritual cleansing and victory into our lives. Remember, the purpose of God in your life isn't your comfort and personal happiness; it is to raise up in your life the image of His Son, Jesus Christ our Lord. God's purpose for you as His son or daughter is inner transformation into the growing reality of His kingdom of the heart. There is profound joy to be found in deepening surrender to that process.

Smooth Stone #5: Being Filled with His Spirit

The final stone to take to defeat this inner giant of temptation is that of being filled anew with the Holy Spirit's presence. It is God's deep desire to have all of us experience the fresh filling of His Spirit on a daily basis. He desires to pour into us the fullness of His love. He wants to pour His power into us, to change us and raise us to newer and higher levels of spiritual life in Christ Jesus. We are as full of the Holy Spirit as we have chosen to be. The fact is, the Lord Jesus has done everything He can do to make this a living reality in our lives. The choice of surrender lies with us. The Christian life is a miracle. It is a human being learning to live crucified to the flesh, the world, and the footholds of the enemy. And it is the human body indwelt by two persons—you and the Holy Spirit!

Please understand, child of God, you and I don't have to cave in to temptation. We don't have to live in sin and continue to commit sins in areas of weakness in our lives. The Lord God sent His Son, Jesus, to rescue us from the clutches of such behaviors. I plead with you: don't fall for the enemy's lies and a milquetoast brand of Christianity that denies God's power to change us. Take your sling of faith and start launching God-ordained projectiles at the inner, enemy-imposed giant of temptation. We don't have to learn to live with it. We can walk with Jesus Christ above it! Every time it comes calling on us, we can throw some stones at it.

Chapter Five

Defeating the Giant of Oppression

I T IS SO IMPORTANT that today's giant-slayers hold fast to
the living Word of God Almighty. The Word of the Lord
is a weapon that can be used against every tactic, scheme,
and method of our enemy Satan. It has clear instructions
regarding the will of God for us and the truth of God that
we can take against the lies of the evil one. The Word of
God is a source of spiritual authority to the child of God.
The Spirit of God anoints it to our hearts and gives us the
ability to confess His truth in every circumstance and to
attack the enemy forces that come against us.

There is no question about this fact: We have been chosen by God to "reign in life through Jesus Christ our Lord"
(Rom. 5:17*b*). Internal giants of the heart are faced and
defeated by the courage and commitment born in our hearts
by faith. Our faith rests in the Word of God and we choose
to believe and act on what He has said He will do over the

enemy's imposition of fear, discouragement, or confusion. Jesus told His disciples—and us, too,

> If you hold to my teaching, you are really my disciples. Then you will know the truth, and the truth will set you free. (John 8:31–32)

The first giants of the heart at which we are looking are those imposed upon us by the wiles of the enemy. We are studying inner giants that are placed in our minds to get us to think things that are contrary to the Word of God. The goal the enemy has is to establish a lie in the human heart, specifically to get us to turn away from the Lord's provisions for our victory. The enemy wants us to remove ourselves from the protective hand of the Father God. He will fight unfairly to get us to the place where we are not trusting the Lord, not claiming and proclaiming His Word over our lives.

Listen closely to the Holy Spirit's whispers to your heart, making the following scriptures come alive with meaning as they relate to defeating inner giants of the heart imposed on us by Satan's beings.

> No, in all these things we are more than conquerors through him who loved us. For I am convinced that neither death nor life, nor angels nor demons, neither the present nor the future, nor any powers, nor height nor depth, nor anything else in all creation, will be able to separate us from the love of God that is in Christ Jesus our Lord. (Rom. 8:37–39)

The weapons we fight with are not the weapons of the world. On the contrary, they have divine power to demolish strongholds. We demolish arguments and every pretension that sets itself up against the knowledge of God, and we take every thought captive and make it obedient to Christ. (2 Cor. 10:3–5)

Notice with me that the Word of the Lord describes the truth that we do, in fact, have a choice in the matter of how we will think and the attitudes we will cherish in our hearts. We don't have to cower in fear or bow down to anything except the Lord God Almighty at the throne of grace. We don't have to put up with lies from the enemy; the apostle Paul calls them pretenses Satan sends to get us to distrust our gracious Master. We can take our thought processes captive and make them obedient to Christ!

Armed with the knowledge of the Word of God as His truth, and buoyed up by faith's attitudes of courage and optimism, let's attack and defeat our second inner giant imposed by the enemy: *oppression.* In referring to this tactic of oppression of the enemy, I am talking about the works of the evil one to burden the child of God with a sense of almost overwhelming heaviness of heart.

The *means* of the oppression can vary from hurtful words from someone we respect, to betrayal by a friend. Oppression can dwell in anything from financial woes or to wounds of the past that are not cleansed and healed by the blood of Jesus.

The *goal* of oppression is to weigh down the believer, to bring about weariness body, heaviness of heart, confusion of mind, and sorrow of soul. Oppression is a favorite tool of the enemy to cause us to make wrong choices when we are in a state of fatigue or frustration, having the effect of turning us away from the Lord, who is our deliverer. When we sense we are being attacked with oppression from the enemy, it is important that we grasp and hold on to several truths:

1. Oppression doesn't necessarily mean there is something wrong with you, that you have sinned or failed God somehow. Quite to the contrary, this is the special tool of the enemy he seems to reserve for choice servants of God in Scripture. Therefore, you may very well be doing—or have the potential to do—many things well in your walk with God by faith, and oppression is a tactic to get you to stop walking with God so well.

2. Oppression has no power over us as children of God unless we permit it. Oppression comes from the outside in. It enters the mind with a view to finding lodging in the heart. The only way oppression can have its desired effect on us is if we take it in and embrace it. If we stand against the initial onslaught of words that cripple and thoughts that harm the heart, oppression has no place of entry.

3. Oppression isn't defeated by introspection or repentance; it is defeated by standing our ground within our heart and mind by faith—by taking thoughts captive and making them obedient to Christ.

Oppression against Heroes of the Faith

Earlier I mentioned that oppression of the enemy seems to be reserved for some of God's most choice servants. There are two men in Scripture—Elijah and John the Baptist—at whom I want us to briefly look as cases in point. These two men who did great exploits for God, opposed the malignant works of the evil one as they walked with God in righteousness, and they experienced incredible oppression from the evil one.

Elijah, you will remember, under the leadership of the Spirit of God, challenged the prophets of Baal to a spiritual battle between Jehovah and Baal on Mount Carmel. It was one prophet of God—standing alone in prayer with a Mighty God—opposed by 450 of the evil one's human instruments, who were under the tutelage of Queen Jezebel, a woman who possessed vast occultic power and influence.

The prophets of Baal were unsuccessful in getting Baal to answer their prayer for fire from heaven. Then, as Elijah repaired the altar of God and had the people drew near to it, the Lord answered Elijah's

> ## The *goal* of oppression is to weigh down the believer, to bring about weariness body, heaviness of heart, confusion of mind, and sorrow of soul.

prayer. The fire of God fell from heaven and consumed the sacrifice on His altar. The people's response was to cry out, "The Lord, he is God." Elijah and the people then destroyed all 450 of those evil priests that had done Jezebel's bidding.

When the queen heard about the death of her prophets, she unleashed powerful curses against Elijah in the name of the gods of darkness whom she served with evil glee. What happened next defies human logic: Elijah had just witnessed the defeat of evil gods by God Almighty, and the prophet had seen God answer his prayers and restore rain to the land. Yet under the oppressive works of darkness, Elijah was powerfully impacted. He ran in fear. He was overwhelmed with fatigue and confusion of mind. He even prayed that the Lord would let him die! This is a classic case of oppression against one of God's chosen instruments. Elijah was in desperate need of the delivering power of God to rescue him from oppression.

Secondly, consider with me the events at the end of John the Baptist's life. He had heard the voice of the Lord God Almighty tell him that the one on whom he saw the Spirit descend in the form of a dove was the Messiah. As he was baptizing Jesus of Nazareth, the heavens opened and the sign he had been given was fulfilled. He had absolute certainty that Jesus was the Son of God, the promised deliverer. He even told some of his best followers to follow Jesus, because he knew he had to decrease and the Lord Jesus was going to increase. Yet, at the end of his life, as he faced his death in Herod's dungeon, he sent some of his disciples to Jesus to ask him, "Are you the one who was to come, or should we expect someone else?" (see Matt. 11:3).

The confusion about something that had been clear in John's mind, points to some kind of tremendously powerful demonic oppression that caused God's special messenger to question what he had previously known with certainty. Jesus sent word back with John's disciples to tell him what they heard and saw, and then he turned to all who were listening and blessed John's role in preparing His way. The Lord knew how powerful the enemy's oppression could be, and He blessed John as an act of grace!

Before I leave this section regarding the enemy oppressing the Lord's choice servants, I want to show you two powerful verses which speak prophetically about the life and ministry our of Lord Jesus.

He was oppressed and afflicted, yet he did not open his mouth; he was led like a lamb to the slaughter, and as a sheep before her shearers is silent, so he did not open his mouth. By oppression and judgment he was taken away. And who can speak of his descendants? For he was cut off from the land of the living; for the transgression of my people was he stricken. (Isa. 53:7–8)

Permit me please, to ask you an honest question. If God the Father permitted His one and only Son Jesus to be oppressed and afflicted by the enemy, doesn't it stand to reason that His adopted sons and daughters would also experience it? Scripture is clear in this regard. The Son of God had no sin of His own; He was completely innocent, and as such, qualified to be our sacrifice. The enemy worked tremendously powerful oppression on Him to get Him to quit. But because He "endured the cross, scorning its shame and sat down at the right hand of the throne of God," you and I have a merciful and faithful High Priest (Heb. 12:2). We, too, can walk in spiritual victory over the oppressive works of the enemy!

A Scriptural View of What Oppression Is and Does

I am thankful the Lord caused the Spirit-inspired authors of the Scriptures to be so open and vulnerable about their experiences of struggling against the enemy. In Psalm 107 there are candid words about a battle with the spiritual oppression of the enemy. The psalmist clearly communicated the ways oppression worked in his life and the feelings he experienced while oppressed. At first glance, the psalm appears to be a psalm of thanksgiving. But upon closer inspection, the psalmist is thanking God for deliverance from oppressive works of darkness that he and others whom he loved had been experiencing. Throughout the text of the psalm, the author uses words like *trouble, distress,* and *affliction.* In verse 39, oppression is specifically mentioned.

Let's consider together how oppression gains entry into the life and what it does when it is in us. First, there are several ways the psalmist points out to us that oppression of the enemy was allowed to gain entry into the lives of people. Some people decided to take their own way and make their own provisions for life. According to verse 4, "they wandered in desert wastelands, finding no way into a city where they could settle." Others chose a more self-centered and sinful approach, as is found in verse 11: "for they had rebelled against the words of God and despised the counsel of the Most High." According to verse 17, those who rebelled against God's Word and ways "became fools through their rebellious ways and suffered affliction because of their iniquities."

Second, notice with me what oppression of the enemy does when it has gained entry into the human heart and life. The heart is made very heavy through the weight of burden. There is within us a type of heartsickness that can be debilitating and, at times, almost overwhelming. The psalmist tells his readers that there's a sense of impending inner death. In verse 18, "they loathed all food and drew near the gates of death." As oppression takes its toll, a type of inner prison lays claim to the human heart. Emotional baggage can and does imprison it's victims. In verses 10–12 and 14 the writer says,

> Some sat in darkness and deepest gloom, prisoners suffering in iron chains, for they had rebelled against the words of God and despised the counsel of the Most High. So he subjected them to bitter labor; they stumbled but there was no one to help. . . . He brought them out of darkness and deepest gloom and broke away their chains.

Third, please take note: the psalmist tells us four times, "Then they cried out to the Lord and He . . ." and then follows those words with the things God did for the oppressed people. God ministered to their lives in saving, redeeming, and delivering works. What the psalmist is teaching is that the only way out of the oppressive works of the evil one in the human heart is to cry out to God in prayer that He will come to His children and set them free. The only way the oppressive works of darkness are destroyed is if God destroys them for us.

As oppression takes its toll, a type of inner prison lays claim to the human heart.

My absolutely most favorite verses in this psalm speak to the healing power of God's redeeming works for His own. I believe these verses can and should be received by the people of God as prophetically referring to the ministry of Jesus Christ our Lord. He is referred to in John 1:14 as the living Word who became flesh and dwelt among us. He came from the Father full of grace and truth.

> Then they cried to the Lord in their trouble, and he saved them from their distress. *He sent forth His Word and healed them; he rescued them from the grave.* Let them give thanks to the Lord for his unfailing love and his wonderful deeds for men. (vss. 19–21, emphasis mine)

Let me remind you again of the fact that this issue of oppression is an act of spiritual warfare. As His soldiers of the cross, we are responsible to stand the ground of our lives He has given to us. We are responsible to take the victory of Jesus Christ our Lord by faith and to claim and proclaim it as our own! We do not have to surrender one inch of ground in our thinking or our desires to the enemy's works of oppression. This inner, enemy-imposed giant can be faced and defeated by the child of God through the power of God.

Giant slayers, we have the whole armor of God available to us. So grab your sling of faith, an attitude of courage, and your shepherd's bag. Let's face this giant of oppression head-on. Walk with me over to the brook, and grab some projectiles to throw by faith, knowing the Lord desires to give us maximum impact on oppression.

Smooth Stone #1: The Word of God
I want to remind you that the truth of God is a weapon in the believing heart and through the believing lips of God's

sons and daughters. When we believe the Word of God and confess it, we unleash God's powerful truth against the lies of the deceiver. Paul taught the Ephesians believers to take unto themselves the whole armor of God (see Eph. 6:13 ff). Several pieces of the armor have to do with the Word of God. The apostle compared the believer's "belt of truth" to the Roman soldier's belt, and the "sword of the Spirit, which is the Word of God" to the soldier's sword.

The truth of the matter is that oppression can be taken captive and destroyed by taking and claiming the Word of God by faith. As the enemy floods us with heaviness, despair, or distress, we can choose to dwell on the majesty of God, worshiping Him in spirit and in truth. There is a wonderful scripture in Isaiah—quoted at the beginning of Jesus' ministry—that is profound when applied to the oppressive works of darkness. Notice that the thoughts and the attitudes we cherish in our hearts are a matter of choice. We can choose truth and praise in the midst of darkness and oppression:

> The Spirit of the Sovereign Lord is on me, because he has anointed me to preach good news to the poor. He has sent me to bind up the brokenhearted, to proclaim freedom for the captives and release from darkness for the prisoners, to proclaim the year of the Lord's favor and the day of vengeance of our God, to comfort all who mourn, and provide for those who grieve in Zion, to bestow on them a crown of beauty instead of ashes, the oil of gladness instead of mourning, and a garment of praise instead of a spirit of despair. They will be called oaks of righteousness, a planting of the Lord for the display of his splendor. (Isa. 61:1–3)

Smooth Stone #2: Brokenness of Heart

He delights in the children of God who choose to be broken in heart and contrite in spirit before Him. He wants to be desired by us. Part of the reason He may permit us to be oppressed by the enemy is to show us how desperately we need Him, His presence, and His power to destroy the works of the enemy. So let oppression bring you to embrace the offering of a broken and contrite heart before God. Decide to embrace the frailty of your humanity instead of propping yourself up in His sight or finding something or someone on which to blame weakness.

Smooth Stone #3: Confessing Our Needs to Him

Offering Him my brokenness and contrition before Him as a worship offering is very special to Him. I'm reminded of so many places in Scripture where the Lord delights in hearing the confession of our need of Him. One of the most special to me is the story, found in Luke 18 of the sinner and the Pharisee praying in the temple. The Pharisee prayed about himself, and because he prayed about himself, he prayed to himself. The sinner humbled himself before God and cried out for mercy. Jesus said that this humble man went home justified before God. Confess your needs before Him with openness and honesty. He awaits and deeply delights in the sincere prayers of His children.

Smooth Stone #4: Drawing Near to Jesus at the Cross

Let me just remind you again, the cross is in the "eternal now" in the heart of the Father. We can meet with Him there, confessing our needs and failings, casting them onto the body of our Lord Jesus, and He takes them away from us. When we come by faith to Him at the cross, we have come to the place of powerful victory over oppression. There at the cross, we are told in Colossians 2:15,

> And having disarmed the powers and authorities, he made a public spectacle of them, triumphing over them by the cross.

Every oppressive spirit of darkness loses its power when God's sons and daughters—in sincere broken and contrite confession—cry out to Jesus at the cross. Let us come boldly to the throne of grace, beholding the Lamb of God who takes away the sin of the world in His body sacrificed on the cross!

Smooth Stone #5: Being Filled with the Holy Spirit

The final stone to throw at the giant of oppression, which really has devastating effects, is inviting the powerful presence of the Holy Spirit to fill us anew. So many of the promises regarding the filling of the Spirit are written in the present, active tense. They are rightly to be translated, "go on being filled with the Holy Spirit." He deeply desires to fill us with His presence and to walk through life with us in sweet fellowship. He Himself will drive the oppressors out of our hearts if we will surrender to Him and invite Him to dwell in us in power!

In closing this chapter, child of God, let me remind you that you can recognize oppression of the heart and mind when it attacks you. Having recognized it, you can defeat it. Take your sling of faith and your God-ordained holy projectiles, and cut oppression down to size in Christ Jesus your Lord! Hear the Spirit speak to you from the Scriptures and *go for it!*

> For though we live in the world, we do not wage war as the world does. The weapons we fight with are not the weapons of the world. On the contrary, they have divine power to demolish strongholds. We demolish arguments and *every pretension that sets itself up against the knowledge of God, and we take captive every thought and make it obedient to Christ.* (2 Cor. 10:3–5, emphasis mine)

Was that thud I just heard the sound of an enemy-imposed giant of the heart hitting the road?

Chapter Six

✍

Defeating the Giant of Worldliness

A S WE HAVE ATTACKED the inner giants of the heart, we have been using the model of the giant-slayers found in Scripture: David, Caleb, Abishai, Sibeccai, Elhanon, and David's nephew Jonathan. Their lives present a tremendous picture to giant-slayers today, regarding what it means to walk with God by faith. We have seen how they put their trust in the Lord, regardless of obstacles in their way. While others chose to allow fear to paralyze them, these men walked with God and did extraordinary exploits for His glory on the earth. They chose God-glorifying faith that enabled them to view all of life through spiritual lenses. They saw obstacles to victorious living as spiritual confrontations of the enemy to their faith, trust, and surrender to God. These men attacked and destroyed their giant-sized obstacles by faith. What a marvelous model for us—people who need to make similar choices today!

The Lord delights in His sons and daughters who love Him and walk with Him in simple childlike trust. He will cover His own with His protective care and will abundantly bless His people who long for intimacy with Him. There are many passages in Scripture in which the Lord God speaks to His people in the first person, regarding His desire to protect, defend, and bless His sons and daughters. Following are some selected verses from Psalm 91, one of my favorite psalms:

> He who dwells in the shelter of the Most High will rest in the shadow of the Almighty. I will say of the Lord, "He is my refuge and my fortress, my God in who I trust." . . .

> He will cover you with his feathers, and under his wings you will find refuge; his faithfulness will be your shield and your rampart. . . .

> If you make the Most High your dwelling, even the Lord, who is my refuge, then no harm will befall you, no disaster will come near your tent. . . .

> "Because he loves me," says the Lord, "I will rescue him; I will protect him, for he acknowledges my name. He will call upon me, and I will answer him: I will be with him in trouble, I will deliver him and honor him. With long life will I satisfy him and show him my salvation."

In this first group of giants, we're looking at those imposed upon us by the enemy. These are things that come from the outside in; they are aimed at getting us to embrace things we know are contrary to the Word of God. These are issues of enemy-inspired attacks against the child of God are designed to get us to make wrong choices that will cause us to drift away from the protective care of the Great Shepherd of the sheep. When the enemy attacks, run to God's heart. Increase your desire to walk in His ways, because you know "the battle is the Lord's and He will deliver us!"

In this chapter we are studying our third giant of the heart imposed upon us by the enemy: *worldliness*. This inner giant is constantly seeking to gain entry points and footholds in us, with a view to impairing our ability and desire to walk with the Lord by faith. Let's take a good look at this world from a biblical perspective and see it for what it really is. The world is definitively the external enemy of God and all that He calls good. Biblically speaking, the sworn enemy of God, Satan, is called the "prince of this world." That in itself should cause the children of God to put up their spiritual guard when it comes to the world in which we live. There are two different Greek words that are translated "the world."

1. The word *oikumene,* which can mean "the populated world" but is often used in Scripture as a metaphor for "the age or philosophical system of thought in which we live." It would be similar to our word *culture*. It is the word found in Romans 12:2 where Paul tells us not to allow the *oikumene* to squeeze us into its mold.

2. The word *kosmos* can mean "the created earth" or "the inhabited world." But it can also mean "a system of thought that runs the inhabited world, a spiritual system of things that is diametrically opposed to God and the kingdom of Jesus Christ our Lord living in people." This would be akin to our word

world. This is the word Jesus used when He described the world as full of hatred toward His disciples on the eve of His crucifixion (see John 15:18; 16:33).

The best written definition I have ever seen that gets at the spiritual connotations of this idea of "the world" is found in Mark Bubeck's book *The Adversary,* which states:

> The world system in its function is a composite expression of the depravity of the flesh of man and the intrigues of Satan's rule combining to oppose the rule of God.

The Inner Giant of Worldliness and God's People

We simply must understand the basic truth of Scripture regarding this external enemy called "the world," which seeks to become an arrogant giant dwelling in our hearts. The world system around us is an insidious enemy of the life of Christ in us. It constantly wages war against our living to please God. It is the very antithesis of the values, ethics, desires, and behaviors we choose as members of the kingdom of Christ Jesus.

> **The world system around us is an insidious enemy of the life of Christ in us.**

The world around us presents moral evil—that which is opposed to God's holiness—as appealing and attractive to the eyes of humankind. It's the same concept that the enemy used on Adam and Eve in the garden, as recorded in Genesis 3:6: "When the woman saw that the fruit of the tree was good for food and pleasing to the eye . . ." Things worldly entice the fleshly nature in order to get us to make sinful choices as though they are in sync with God's revealed truth. Yet please hear the truth—that the world hates Christ and His people—under the guidance of your inner Counselor, the Holy Spirit:

> If the world hates you keep in mind that it hated me first. If you belonged to the world, it would love you as its own. As it is you do not belong to the world, but I have chosen you out of the world. (John 15:18–19)

The apostle Paul gave us a tremendous word of teaching about our making choices regarding the enticement of the world system around us. In Romans 12:1–2, Paul wrote:

> Therefore, I urge you brothers, in view of God's mercy, to offer your bodies as living sacrifices, holy and pleasing to God—this is your spiritual act of worship. Do not conform any longer to the pattern of this world, but be transformed by the renewing of your mind. Then you will be able to test and approve what God's will is—his good, pleasing and perfect will.

The world system promises joy and happiness in the things it offers us in the here and now. The world offers us things, such as the goal of materialistic happiness in money, cars, and salaries. It offers satisfaction of our appetites for food, prestige, or sexual gratification. It offers joy in the better job, in the bigger firm, with a higher profile and more people to manage and bigger bucks and perks. The world system promises all of this and delivers on none of it, because it is a hollow illusion created by the "father of lies."

The apostle John wrote a scripture that talks about the world in specific and concrete terms, the meaning of which is hard to miss. To give spiritual significance to this world, to love the world is like hugging a poisonous snake. As we embrace it, we embrace our own harm and a slow death of paralysis of our nervous system. In the same way, to love the world is to invite death to godly desires in our heart. Listen to the Spirit of God counsel us from 1 John 2:15–17:

> Do not love the world or anything in the world. If anyone loves the world the love of the Father is not in him. For everything in the world—*the cravings of sinful man, the lust of the eyes, the boasting of what he has and does*—comes not from the Father, but from the world. The world and its desires pass away, but the man who does the will of God lives forever. (emphasis mine)

The counsel of Scripture is this: don't attach spiritual significance to anything in this world. This giant of the heart is extremely sneaky. Its insidious nature is in its ability to creep into us without our noticing its presence. Worldliness seeks to gain entry points to our hearts and minds, then it seeks to get footholds, and ultimately it will try to control us through desires for what is contrary to the will of God. Only after it is in us does it clamor for satisfaction. On the way into our lives it postures itself as pleasing and controllable.

When giant of worldliness is permitted in our lives, things begin ruling us, and we live under the tyranny of getting and accomplishing. It seeks to consume our time and energy with the temporal and hollow illusion of inner satisfaction through earthly gain. It promises peace and pleasure but delivers pressure, stressful loads, hurts, and hatred in interpersonal relationships. Ultimately, the world system will enslave us with the slow and methodical tyranny of sinful cravings for appetite satisfaction.

The apostle Paul wrote about a man named Demas who allowed the internal giant of worldliness to seduce him: "Demas, because he loved this world has deserted me" (2 Tim. 4:10).

We Christians have notoriously attempted to reduce the giant of worldliness to simple equations and lists of rules. This elusive giant is so insidious with its new enticements, that it really defies such a simplistic and systemic approach. We may keep a long list of rules, doing these things and not doing those things, and yet still be quite worldly in our hearts and desires regarding money, property, etc. This is essentially a matter of the heart—a matter of which desires I choose to fan into flame in my life. If I am desiring to get more of life's trinkets and toys, and this pursuit is cutting away some of my desire to please God, I am worldly. The inner giant lives in me!

> **Ultimately, the world system will enslave us with the slow and methodical tyranny of sinful cravings for appetite satisfaction.**

The World's Consistent Hatred of Christ and His People

I take you back to the words of our Lord Jesus, spoken to His disciples on the eve of His crucifixion. Christ taught His people just how hostile this world system is to Him and, consequently, to us because the Spirit of Jesus lives in us!

> If the world hates you, keep in mind that it hated me first. If you belonged to the world, it would love you as its own. As it is, you do not belong to the world, but I have chosen you out of the world. That is why the world hates you. (John 15:18–19)

The enemy has devised this world's philosophical system as the antithesis of all that God our Father calls righteous, holy, and good. The enemy wants the giant of the worldly to become an inner giant of the heart so that people are robbed of time and energy with which to love and worship God the Father, Son, and Spirit. We ourselves aren't desired by the enemy; Satan's desires are stealing glory from God and putting people in bondage.

We must understand a second thing about this giant of worldliness. There are two natures living in us as the people of God. There is a human nature in us, and there is His divine nature in us by His Holy Spirit. The nature we feed, grows strong and controls us. The nature we starve, dies and loses control over us. The issue of feeding the nature of God with faith and surrender is never stagnant in us. It is a living dynamic in us that ebbs and flows like a stream. The apostle John wrote another paragraph about defeating the world in the provisions of Jesus, who overcame the world (see John 16:33). John's verbs describing faith that overcomes the world are written in the present, indicative, active tense. These should be correctly read, "the ones who believe and go on believing every day."

> This is love for God: to obey his commands. And his commands are not burdensome, for everyone born of

God overcomes the world. This is the victory that has overcome the world, even our faith. Who is it that overcomes the world? Only he who believes that Jesus is the Son of God. (1 John 5:3–5)

Too many of God's sons and daughters do not recognize this key issue regarding our faith being a living, growing dynamic of life. Too often we tend to run on yesterday's blessings and provisions and do not renew ourselves in the Lord Jesus on a daily basis. Consequently, the insidious enemy—the giant of worldliness—creeps into us slowly, enticing the fleshly to sinful satisfaction of appetites. We sometimes don't recognize what has happened to us for days, weeks, or even months.

In Psalm 101:1–4, God used our giant-slayer-turned-king, David, to teach me some things about the giant of worldliness. As I was reading the Scriptures one day, God gave me three principles I want to remember about choosing to refresh myself in the Lord and to renew my faith in Him daily, standing my ground against the inner giant of worldliness. Let me share them with you.

PRINCIPLE #1

I will choose to live a life of godliness in my own home, behind closed doors with those who know me best. Verse 2 of Psalm 101 says, "I will walk in my house with a blameless heart." What David essentially says here is "Whether people can see me or not, I long to be blameless in the sight of God. That is a choice regarding passions I will feed in my own heart."

PRINCIPLE #2

I will choose not to view vileness that entices my fleshly desires to be satisfied through sins of my mind or body.

Verse 3 says, "I will set before my eyes no vile thing." People of God, in these days of sexual promiscuity and immorality that is portrayed in the media as good and entertaining, we need to choose to make a covenant with our own eyes not to look at impure videos under the guise of entertainment. The argument "It is in the privacy of my own home, and I am an adult who can handle it" just doesn't wash with Scripture. First, we defile our own heart and feed our eyes with looking wrongly. Second, we force God to watch something filthy with us because He lives in our body and sees with our eyes. Third, we open our home and our family members to spiritual influences of the giant of worldliness. We need to deal drastically—at the cross of Jesus by faith—with the desire of our heart to see garbage.

> The people with whom you choose to invest time in this life will have an affect on your life.

PRINCIPLE #3

I will choose to disassociate myself from people who do what God tells me to stay away from. In verses 3b–4 we read, "The deeds of faithless men I hate; they will not cling to me. Men of perverse heart shall be far from me; I will have nothing to do with evil." Choose your closest companions well. The people with whom you choose to invest time in this life will have an affect on your life. Make sure they are people of character, or they won't better you!

We have armed ourselves with the truth regarding how to recognize this giant. We have learned about how it seeks to stealthily gain access to our hearts. Walk with me by faith into the valleys of the heart. Let's take the sling of faith and head over to the brook to select the five smooth stones we are going to use as projectiles. Let's have maximum impact in our internal battle against this giant of the heart, worldliness!

Smooth Stone #1: The Word of God

There are several things about the defeat of this inner giant of worldliness that we can learn from clear teachings of Scripture. First and foremost, our Lord Jesus Christ took on the giant of the world and defeated it for us. He told His disciples He had done so even before He went to the cross for humankind:

> I have told you these things, so that in me you may have peace. In this world you will have trouble. But take heart! I have overcome the world. (John 16:33)

Second, being a biblical overcomer of the giant of worldliness is a matter of choosing a higher love in my heart. Paul told the believers in Rome that the world would not squeeze them into its mold if they would go on offering themselves up to God daily in spiritual acts of worship. Choosing to love God supremely will keep the love of the world out. The love of God will keep us where rules and regulations cannot take us! Listen to the Spirit make Romans 12:2 come alive to us, regarding defeating this giant of the heart in the victory of Jesus Christ:

> Do not conform any longer to the pattern of this world, but be transformed by the renewing of your mind. Then

you will be able to test and approve what God's will is—
his good, pleasing and perfect will.

Our job is to fan into flame the love of God in our hearts,
to be people of private worship and adoration of Him. We
are to continue being renewed daily by His Word made alive
in us by His Spirit. His higher love in us will keep us desir-
ous of pleasing Him and of walking in His good, pleasing,
and perfect will. That will put some serious damage on the
forehead of the giant of worldliness.

Smooth Stone #2: Brokenness of Heart

Where we see that this giant has crept into us we need
to own up to the fact that our will has been involved somewhere along the way. When we see this giant has begun to
stand in our hearts, clamoring for its ways, we must permit
the Spirit of God to produce brokenness of heart in us so
we can see from His perspective how it got there. We must
allow the sorrow we feel to bring us a desire for His remedial action in our lives.

Smooth Stone #3: Confession of Our Need

Allowing Him to break our hearts and embracing the
message of brokenness is a necessary first step. The second
is of equal importance to Him: He wants us to own how the
giant of the world was permitted to set up shop in our hearts
and minds. He wants us to confess our needs and bring
them out into the light, because He desperately wants us to
mature—that is, not to make the same mistakes again and
again. Tell Him what you see in yourself and what you need
from Him of His provisions of grace, peace and mercy.

Smooth Stone #4: Drawing Near to Him at the Cross

He desires for us to meet with Him by faith at the cross of Jesus. God's method for dealing with what offends Him, is to destroy it at the cross of Christ. There at the cross, what is in us that is displeasing to God is placed by faith into the bosom of Jesus, and He bears those things away from us. The apostle Paul wrote a word in his letter to the Galatians that is powerful, regarding destroying the fresh entry points, or footholds, of the inner giant of worldliness:

> May I never boast except in the cross of our Lord Jesus Christ, through which the world has been crucified to me, and I to the world. (Gal. 6:14)

If we find the garbage desires of this world living in us, the inner giant of worldliness clamoring for sinful satisfaction of human appetites, let's decide to take it to the cross. It has been crucified in the body of our Lord Jesus sacrificed for us on the cross. It therefore has no power over us unless we permit it!

Smooth Stone #5: Being Filled Anew with the Holy Spirit

It is the deep desire of God the Father to fill His sons and daughters with His Holy Spirit. He longs to come to us and give to us His desires, passions, and power to live them. There is an awesome Scripture regarding how the Holy Spirit desires to make us overcomers of the giant of worldliness. Paul was writing to one of his sons in the faith in the Book of Titus 2:11–12:

> For the grace of God that brings salvation has appeared to all men. It teaches us to say "No" to ungodliness and

worldly passions and to live self-controlled, upright and godly lives in this present age.

If those things are His will—and they are—then we can believe He will give us the power of His Spirit to carry His will to completion.

I am thoroughly convinced the Lord has defeated the giant of worldliness for the believers. He wants us to walk in His victory over every aspect of the enemy's darkness. Our choice in the matter is crucial. Will we love God more passionately from the heart and surrender to Him daily as living sacrifices to Him? Will we invite the Holy Spirit to dwell in us in power and make the life and victory of Jesus Christ our Lord personal in us?

The more I learn to know Him and walk in His ways, the more ugly the things of this world look to me. What loves and desires will we feed and nourish, children of God? Will we love what is destined to become rust and dust? Or will we desire what cannot be measured by the standards used in this world? Will we desire to invest in a kingdom that is out of this world?

Whiz, splat, thud. Is it just me, or is your accuracy with your sling of faith getting better?

Chapter Seven

⚭

Defeating the Giant
of Adversity

THE LORD GOD HAS REACHED to the human heart with His precious gift of faith, which He wants us in turn to embrace and give back to Him. When we trust in Him as faithful God, He delights in us and ministers to us with His keeping, protective, and jealous care. The believer's attitudes that all of us so desperately need are courage and optimism. As I think about the attitudes born of faith, the one person who comes to mind immediately is the shepherd boy David. This teenage boy loved and worshiped God with all of his heart. He wrote love songs to God, many of which are preserved for us in the Psalms. Here was a young man who had conquered the internal battlefields of the heart. Out of his inner walk with God, he entered the battlefield, in the name of the Lord, to do battle with a giant-sized killing machine named Goliath.

David had the heart of a victor. He chose to believe God, and the attitudes of faith, courage, and optimism flowed from his deep understanding of God's faithfulness and promises to him. Goliath had been shouting his boast that it really wasn't a fair fight because David was just a boy. David, in essence, said, "You are right! This isn't a fair fight at all. You are in big trouble because God is against you!" Listen to his testimony of trust in God, even before the battle with Goliath began:

> You come against me with sword and spear and javelin, but I come against you in the name of the Lord Almighty, the God of the armies of Israel, whom you have defied. This day the Lord will hand you over to me, and I'll strike you down and cut off your head. Today I will give the carcasses of the Philistine army to the birds of the air and the beasts of the earth, and the whole world will know that there is a God in Israel. All those gathered here will know that it is not by sword or spear that the Lord saves; for the battle is the Lord's and he will give all of you into our hands. (1 Sam. 17:45–48)

As we attack the giants of the heart, it is important that we choose to walk with God by faith. The victory depends on who God is and what He has decided He will do. It is not dependent on our resources or lack thereof. We must arm ourselves with the truth of God's Word. Let's choose to believe Him regardless of our circumstances, to be buoyed by faith's attitudes of courage and optimism. Let's go after our fourth enemy-imposed giant of the heart: *adversity*. It is a fact of life, as well as clear biblical truth, that sometimes life is painful and incredibly unfair. Adversity is no respecter of persons. It will strike us all, at times, with extremely hard circumstances.

Adversity will often strike us in the context of our human relationships. The cost of loving people is that they will hurt us sometimes. When you truly love, you become vulnerable to being hurt. Often emotional pain is experienced through loving another deeply, only to experience rejection or the sting of being unfairly criticized. Adversity often strikes our family relationships through such things as financial strains, physical suffering, the bitterness of divorce, and sometimes even physical death of a young family member.

Having been a pastor for twenty years, I have seen more than my share of adversity strike the lives of people. I've walked with numerous families that have disintegrated. I've stood beside the graves of teenagers and have cried buckets of tears with people. One of the most painful was when our Bible-quizzing team was in a terrible automobile accident on their way to a quiz tournament in Canada. Several families were touched with adversity. Two teens were badly injured. Jason Rosado, a fourteen-year-old boy who walked with Jesus, died from head injuries. His parents, Carlos and Ruth, were one of our deacon couples in our church family. Adversity struck a wonderful family with ultimate tragedy. I watched them grieve and weep for years as a man and woman of God.

Don't tell me life is always fair to us if we'll just walk with God. Scripture teaches us this life is about getting ready for the next one, and we should live well so we can die well. It is definitely not about our comfortable American dream. Personally, I have seen too many dreams die far too early to believe the American form of the Gospel we so often hear today.

The Scriptures give us many principles both to understand and to deal righteously with adversity when it strikes
us. God desires us to live victoriously regardless of our circumstances. Scripture teaches us that Satan is the author of
adversity and hardships with the goal of creating bitterness
in us through suffering. God's desire in permitting adversity to strike His people, is to walk through the adversity
with us, causing it to become for us the refiner's fire, making us better, more mature disciples of Christ. We choose
the outcome of our adverse circumstances by deciding to
whom we will turn when life hurts!

Adversity Can Be a Messenger of Grace

The apostle Paul understood about adverse circumstances and the fact that they can not be permitted to rule
over us. This man loved the Lord Jesus with all of his heart,
soul, mind, and strength. He went after the will of God
wholeheartedly. He was opposed by human beings and demonic beings. He was beaten, imprisoned, stoned and left
for dead, hungry, shipwrecked, and bitten by poisonous
snakes. Allow the Spirit of God to teach you from Paul's
words in 2 Corinthians 4:7–11:

> But we have this treasure in jars of clay to show that this
> all-surpassing power is from God and not from us. We
> are hard pressed on every side, but not crushed; per-
> plexed, but not in despair; persecuted, but not aban-
> doned; struck down, but not destroyed. We always carry
> around in our body the death of Jesus, so that the life of
> Jesus may also be revealed in our body. For we who are
> alive are always being given over to death for Jesus' sake,
> so that his life may be revealed in our mortal body.

The overwhelming weight of truth Paul wanted his readers to grasp is to own the fact that adversity strikes us all as part of our human experience. Because we are subject to human frailty and sin's grip, we are powerless to deal with life victoriously. Human weakness must be owned and confessed to God, who alone is self-sufficient.

What a word to our culture of self-sufficient people who seem to buy into the lie of rugged individualism, evidenced by our plethora of best-selling self-help books we swallow hook, line, and sinker. The truth of the matter is, I can't make it on my own. I need His help to live a life of joy and victory. We all need to find the place that Paul—along with thousands of believers down through the ages—found in Christ.

> **We choose the outcome of our adverse circumstances by deciding to whom we will turn when life hurts!**

> I know what it is to be in need, and I know what it is to have plenty. I have learned the secret of being content in any and every situation, whether well fed or hungry, whether living in plenty or in want. I can do everything through him who gives me strength. (Phil. 4:12–13)

In order to bring us to the end of our self-sufficiency, the all-sufficient Lord God Almighty will permit His special sons and daughters to go through periods of adversity. Some of God's heroes of the faith have called these experiences "the dark night of the soul." (These are, I think, taken from Jesus' words to His closest followers in Matthew 10). One such hero of the faith, Oswald Chambers, wrote the following:

> At times God puts us through the discipline of darkness to teach us to heed Him. "What I tell you in the darkness"—watch where God puts you into darkness and when you are there keep your mouth shut. Are you in dark circumstances just now? Then remain quiet. If you open your mouth in the dark you will talk in the wrong mood: Darkness is the time to listen. Don't talk to people about it or read books on darkness; listen and heed. If you talk to other people you can't hear what God is saying. When you are in the darkness, listen, and God will give you a very precious message.

> **In order to bring us to the end of our self-sufficiency, the . . . Lord God Almighty will permit His special sons and daughters to go through periods of adversity.**

Chambers captured something I don't think we know much about here in North America. We'd do well to understand and be grasped by this truth: *God is much more concerned with my character develop-*

ment than He is with my comfort! In our culture, we value comfort—the good life—but in the eyes of God, the good life is a life in which He, we, and others can see the growing image of Jesus Christ in us!

The truth of the matter is that every person God has mightily used on planet earth to advance His kingdom, has been taken into the "school of God"—into a place where they are alone with the Lord in the desert. These are barren, arid places where we must learn to trust Him for His provisions of grace, no matter what may come. Moses, Elijah, John the Baptist, and our Lord Jesus all have in common the desert experiences with the Father. Human weakness is owned and confessed in the desert. Trust in the Lord's provisions is put to the test in the desert.

Adversity in the lives of God's people today is analogous to the desert experiences of God's people in Scripture. In the desert experiences God disciplines us, with the goal being our ultimate maturity as His sons and daughters. Adversity can, therefore, be a messenger of grace to those who have eyes to see it.

Biblical Examples of Victory in the Midst of Adversity

The first biblical example of a life of spiritual victory in the midst of the enemy's imposition of adversity in his life is Job. Job experienced the tragedy of all of his children being killed in the collapse of a house. He had all of his wealth stripped away, and his crops and livestock were destroyed. He experienced incredible suffering in his body and then was treated to the stinging rebuke of his wife who told him, "Curse God and die." The capper to the whole thing was when his three buddies showed up and spent many hours with him, accusing him of secret malicious sin.

103

Many people reading the Book of Job miss the key point of the book when they draw the erroneous conclusion that the primary lesson he was being taught was patience. You have probably heard the old adage He has the patience of Job. I don't believe that is the primary lesson God wants His children to receive when we study Job's life. It is not an issue of learning to be patient. Rather, it is learning to trust God's heart of love and grace when life hurts so much you don't think you can go on. The real issue in Job's heart was the issue of faith in who God is that produced patience in suffering.

The second biblical example that comes to mind regarding trusting God in the midst of adversity is God's man Daniel. Here was a young man who was taken from his home and carried into exile. He was taken from his mother and father and every support system he had ever known. He witnessed horrible destruction and violence in the city of Jerusalem. He was raised to a position of favor in the service of King Darius, only to be accused of treachery and wickedness, because of his love for and devotion to God. Knowing the king's edict to not pray to anyone other than the king, Daniel went to his room, opened his windows toward Jerusalem, and talked to God anyway. He chose to become a candidate for lion food rather than reject his prayer life of adoring God. His deep faith in the Lord flowed out of his heart—both before and after the lion's-den experience.

As the king arrived at the lion's den in the morning he asked Daniel, "Daniel, has your God whom you serve continually been able to rescue you from the lions?"

Daniel responded, "O king, my God is able and has sent his angels to shut the lion's mouths" (see Dan. 6:20–22).

The previous night, Darius had worshiped the law of the land. But in the morning, loving Jehovah was the law of the land. This happened because one young man, hundreds of miles away from home, trusted in God's heart of love and mercy when life was painful.

As a third biblical model of a person who definitely faced and defeated his share of adversity consider the life of the apostle Paul. Let me remind you of his testimony in 2 Corinthians 4:7, which we mentioned earlier: "We have this treasure in jars of clay to show that the all surpassing power is from God and not from us."

The Lord is looking to bless those who will trust Him no matter what life throws at them. Paul was one such man who endured under incredible difficulty—no matter what. We endure in adversity by staying fixed on who God is and what His purposes are for our lives as revealed in Scripture. Paul wrote later in 2 Corinthians 4:17, "For our light and momentary troubles are achieving for us an eternal glory that far outweighs them all." Paul stayed at it because he was fixed on both the presence of God in his heart and the purpose of God for his life.

As I close out this section of biblical examples of people who believed God regardless of adversity, please allow me to share one more thing with you. There is an obscure Scripture in Peter's writing that cuts across the grain of our North American, watered-down version of the gospel of Jesus. There is a gospel preached here in our culture that sounds like, but is different from, scriptural Christianity. The essence of this gospel is the message, "You deserve the best because you are a child of God." Peter wrote a word about suffering adversity in 1 Peter 4:19: "So then, those who suffer according to God's will should commit themselves to their faithful Creator and continue to do good." I haven't heard many sermons on that one lately.

If we are going to defeat the giant of adversity that stands in the valleys of life, bellowing at us, "You can't beat me," we are going to need the Lord's help. We need the Word as a weapon and His mighty anointing of His Spirit to apply it. It is time to grab your sling and your shepherd's bag and head over to the brook with me to pick out the five smooth stones we're going to need.

Smooth Stone #1: The Word of God

If we are to beat the giant of adversity, we are going to need to know the Word of God for our lives personally. We must know His provisions and His plans for us if we are to be able to persevere through adverse circumstances. We must have a perspective of life that is bigger than what we can humanly see. We need to come to the throne of grace and get God's viewpoint. There are tremendous words of promised future blessings in Scripture that the Lord will make very personal to us if we will but ask Him to do so. Knowing He is walking with us—as He did with the three Hebrew boys in the fiery furnace and with Daniel in the lion's den—permits us to look for His purpose and work in our character development through our experiences of adversity:

> For I know the plans I have for you, declares the Lord, plans to prosper you and not to harm you, plans to give you a hope and a future. Then you will call upon me and come and pray to me, and I will listen to you. You will seek me and find me when you seek me with all your heart. I will be found by you, declares the Lord. (Jer. 29:11–14a)

Therefore, we do not lose heart. Though outwardly we are wasting away, yet inwardly we are being renewed day by day. For our light and momentary troubles are achieving for us an eternal glory that far outweighs them all. So we fix our eyes not on what is seen, but on what is unseen. For what is seen is temporary, but what is unseen is eternal. (2 Cor. 4:16–18)

Smooth Stone #2: Brokenness of Heart

Knowing the love of God, that He will never leave us nor forsake us, permits us to take the posture of permitting adversity to bring us greater, deeper levels of brokenness before Him. Adversity, when viewed as a messenger of grace, can be seen as the permissive will of God to bring out deeper maturity in our lives. As mentioned before, God is more concerned about the development of our character than He is with our comfort. We can allow brokenness to speak the messages to our soul, our heart, and our mind that we can hear only when our heart aches. We must permit brokenness to have its way and to draw us away from our human ways, thoughts, and self-preserving actions.

Smooth Stone #3: Confession of Our Need

Having experienced brokenness of heart before the Lord, we can go on to talk out with Him how we are feeling. We can bring out into the light of His love the hurt of the adverse circumstances and the things in our life, our heart, and our mind that suffering in adversity has permitted us to see. When we tell Him everything we are seeing, the enemy cannot use it against us as a tool reserved in the darkness of our inner closets. The Lord already knows it, but confession gets it out into the light, which is best for our transformation! Knowing something is true and believing that it is so is good. Confessing verbally, however, is better because words have spiritual power. They communicate the heart of every matter before God and aid in the destruction of enemy-devised patterns of hiding things.

Smooth Stone #4: Drawing Near to Jesus at the Cross

The Lord Jesus has already died our death for us on the cross. He has already crucified sin, death, and all the powers of hell on our behalf. The only thing we are responsible to do is to believe that what He has done for us is sufficient for our personal deliverance—that God accepts His works for me. When I know this to be truth, I come to the cross of Jesus, by faith, and lay in His bosom everything that is in me or around me that is offensive to God. My gracious Master, Jesus, takes these things from me and, in return, gives me His grace, mercy, forgiveness, and the gift of His righteousness.

Smooth Stone #5: The Fresh Filling of the Holy Spirit

As He comes to live in me in greater measure, as He sets my heart on fire and anoints me, I am empowered to live above my circumstances. I am given grace from within that holds me steady, regardless of the outer pressures of life, problems, and adversities. The Holy Spirit of God Almighty living in me keeps a constant inner pressure pushing outward, while the enemy, the world, and circumstances try to cause me to cave inward. Listen one more time to the Holy Spirit's inner counsel to you from Paul's words to the Corinthian believers:

> But we have this treasure in jars of clay to show that this all-surpassing power is from God and not from us. We

are *hard pressed on every side, but not crushed; perplexed, but not in despair.* (2 Cor. 4:7–8, emphasis mine)

What kept Paul's clay pot from being crushed though he was hard pressed? It was the presence of the Spirit of Christ Jesus living in Him. What will keep your clay pot from being crushed by the hurtful circumstances of adversity? I trust you'll throw the fifth stone at the forehead of the giant of adversity!

Part Three

Giants of the Heart We Impose on Ourselves

Chapter Eight

❧

Defeating the Giant
of Bitterness

IT IS IMPORTANT THAT WE hold the truth of the Word of God in our thinking. We have been given the awesome privilege of choosing the attitudes with which we will face life. We are told in the Word of God we have been given authority to reign in life through Jesus Christ our Lord. The Word of God believed, received under the Spirit's counsel, and confessed through lips of faith, is powerful for the tearing down of strongholds of hopelessness in the human heart and mind.

All too often we treat our inner giants of the heart the way David's brothers and the rest of Saul's army treated Goliath. The giant-sized problem stood out in the valley shouting his defiance at them, "You can't beat me!" And they hid in the rocks hoping desperately the giant would go away. What we need is the same courage born of faith that David, our teenage shepherd-boy-turned-giant-slayer, used to attack Goliath. We choose to face and defeat, these inner giants of the heart through our faith in Christ Jesus. As we do we find ourselves growing in freedom, peace, and intimacy with the Lord.

We must remember how internal and external giants are defeated today. We are more than conquerors in Christ Jesus our Lord. In Revelation 12, we are taught that we overcome by the blood of the Lamb, the word of our testimony, and by not loving this life so much as to shrink from death to what imprisons us. Listen to the words the Holy Spirit gave Paul to pass on to the Corinthians as they faced giants of the heart:

> But we have this treasure in jars of clay to show that the all-surpassing power is from God and not from us. (2 Cor. 4:7)

> The weapons we fight with are not the weapons of the world. On the contrary, they have divine power to demolish strongholds. We demolish arguments and every pretension that sets itself up against the knowledge of God, and we take captive every thought and make it obedient to Christ. (2 Cor. 10:3–5)

Now there was a man who knew very well from whence comes the power to be more than a conqueror of the inner giants of his heart. Meeting life's hardships, demands and giant-sized obstacles with faith and confidence in the provisions of Jesus Christ our Lord is our only hope. He will give us victory and lead us to attitudes of faith, confidence, optimism, and courage, regardless of problems or obstacles. Our part in this equation is to turn away from the world's value of self-help and rugged individualism. The resources

I have, or what I lack, will never result in my freedom of heart. As we learn to walk with the Lord and know His heart of love for us, He will deliver us, manifest His power to cleanse us, and demonstrate Himself as holy and awesome through us in increasing measures. Remember, the real issue of our deliverance is never the power of God to change me. It is really my willingness to see my need of Him, my longing to be changed by Him, and my appropriating by faith what He has told me He will do.

> No, in all these things we are more than conquerors through him who loved us. For I am convinced that neither death nor life, neither angels nor demons, neither the present nor the future, nor any powers, neither height nor depth, nor anything else in all creation, will be able to separate us from the love of God that is in Christ Jesus our Lord. (Rom. 8:37–39)

Armed with the truth of God's Word to us and buoyed up by faith's optimism and courage, let's get after this first self-imposed giant of the heart: *bitterness.* This giant can and often does grip God's people, defeating us from within if we aren't on guard and watchful for its entrance and growth in our hearts. Bitterness, when present in us, affects the heart, soul, and spirit and can have tremendously debilitating effects on the physical body. The giant of bitterness in the human heart has roots that sink deeply into the soul like tentacles of an octopus. These roots are often in offenses or wounds inflicted on us earlier in life, which in turn, caused deep internal hurt to grow and expand over time. Bitterness is often entertained and permitted to grow because we have not taken the wounds and painful memories to the cross.

We have not dealt with them in the precious provisions Jesus our Lord died to make available to us. The hurt is held instead of released into the bosom of Jesus, cleansed, and forgiven so that healing grace might flow into us from His heart of love.

This important principle cannot be overstated: *Bitterness is rooted in assuming our right to feel hurt as opposed to our throne-room privileges to deal with our hurts, wounds, or offenses at the cross of Jesus.*

Look with me at two verses of scripture that expose the devastating power of bitterness, not only in the life of wounded persons but also in the lives of their acquaintances.

> Make every effort to live in peace with all men and to be holy: without holiness no one will see the Lord. See to it that no one misses the grace of God and that no bitter root grows up to cause trouble and defile many. (Heb. 12:14–15)

Please notice what bitterness does to the individual:

1. *Physical Disorders.* Almost all of us can see bitterness on the face of a person who bears it. It causes many physical symptoms and can even cut short the life of a person. A bitter person is often mean, harshly critical, and judgmental—a boiling pot of negative emotions waiting to erupt.
2. *Psychological Illnesses.* Things, such as anxiety attacks, stomach disorders (including ulcers and excess acidic output), eating disorders of various kinds,

even nervous breakdowns, can come as a result of not having dealt with old wounds and offenses.

Also notice what can and does often happen as bitterness touches others in community with the wounded one:

1. *Causes Trouble.* Because of its critical nature, negative emotions, and judgmental attitudes, bitterness is constantly on the attack. Bitterness of heart can be a reason behind relational problems with others whom we love the most. Often the marriages, family, church member,

> **The giant of bitterness in the human heart has roots that sink deeply into the soul like tentacles of an octopus.**

and coworker relationships we are presently in are harmed by old unresolved offenses. Bitterness can cause trouble in the community of faith by dividing people against each other. The offense spreads to others, and people choose up sides over the hurt.

2. *Defiles Many.* Because it is an internal boiling cauldron of negative emotion, bitterness constantly splashes out on other people. It is like an erupting volcano that isn't capable of being harnessed. It just cannot be confined to the heart in which it lives. It

will, invariably, find the path of least resistance to the surface. Bitterness of heart does, in fact, defile many because it involuntarily escapes from the wounded person's mouth!

For me, one of the most difficult things to deal with in regards to bitterness is that often those who have permitted it to gain entry in them are unaware of its presence. They often don't even know why they are bitter. Their self-perception is "this is just the way I am." In reality, the Word of God teaches us that, as His sons and daughters, we don't have to stay the way we are, because of who Jesus is and what He has done for us on the cross!

Bitterness Is a Result of Our Choices

In the verses to which I alluded earlier from Hebrews 12, there are some specific and well-chosen words there that really speak to the issue of why bitterness remains in the human heart. The author says to us, "You make every effort to live in peace with all men"; "You make every effort to be holy" (even in your relationships with people); "You see to it that no one misses the grace of God" (which means we are to seek to show others His grace as He gives it to us).

"You see to it that no bitter root grows up." The first choice we make, to which the author points us in this text, is that we definitely have a choice in the matter as to whether or not we will permit bitterness to enter our lives, grow in us, and flow out of us. We choose how we will deal with the issues that cause us pain. When adversity strikes us or we suffer an injustice, we all make choices as to how we will handle this on the inside. When I'm feeling hurt, God understands it. In fact, He has permitted this to happen, so there must be some way He will make this to serve His purposes in me. In Hebrews 4:14–16, we are taught that the Lord Jesus is our Great High Priest who is "able to sympathize with our weaknesses." He is able to feel our heartaches and pain. He offers us "grace and mercy for our times of need at His throne of grace." Our Master is our model and He understands how it feels to bear injustice and be hurt by people whom we love.

> **Bitterness of heart does, in fact, defile many because it involuntarily escapes from the wounded person's mouth!**

Yet when bitterness has taken root, the initial thing we have done to allow it is to forsake God's offer of grace to help us endure the pain. The words above are "See to it that no one misses the grace of God." Grace is available to us when we suffer injustice in righteousness, and that grace enables us to offer love and forgiveness to the offenders. Don't miss this gracious offer from your Provider! Yet this is often what we do. We choose to forsake His grace and, instead, embrace what we consider our inalienable rights as North Americans—to be hurt and offended! Rather than forgiving others, we choose to be hurt, bear our hurts, share our hurts with others, and expand the wounds over time. This clinging to our rights to be hurt is the exact opposite attitude the apostle Paul told the Philippians and all believers to maintain:

> Your attitude should be the kind that was shown us by
> Jesus Christ, who, though he was God, did not demand
> and cling to his rights as God, but laid aside his mighty
> power and glory, taking the disguise of a slave and becoming like men. (Phil. 2:5–6 TLB)

Choice number two in the downward spiral away from grace and toward bitterness is to decide to embrace feelings of resentment at the offense what was unjustly done to us, and choosing to feel resentment toward the offender. We embrace negative feelings toward the one who did the hurting. If it isn't quickly arrested in the heart, resentment can cause a good deal more damage than the original wound. When we choose to embrace this in our hearts, the original wound expands and grows in its power and intensity. Often over time, the wound is no longer the issue. Resentment doesn't allow us to stay focused on the issue. We have a problem with so-and-so as a person. "Do you know what so-and-so did to me?" degenerates to "Do you know what so-and-so is really like?" Now the inner feelings have taken on a life of their own and will eventually lead to full-scale hatred and retaliation against the offender.

Choice number three, in the downward spiral away from grace is the choice to embrace bitterness. This is, in effect, the nursing of the wound, the heartache it has caused, and the unforgiveness and resentment it has birthed. Bitterness will manifest itself through anger, hatred, and even retaliation. And the really nice packaging in which we try to conceal our bitter words and actions is the self-justifying argument that it is, of course, all the fault of the person who hurt us. We have a right to be the victim here! We feel this way because of what they did to us, and we want them to really feel what they've done to us. Let them come to us and repent for their issues, then maybe we'll forgive them.

The Reversal of the Process of Bitterness

The problem with the growth of bitterness is that the Lord doesn't see it this way at all. His ways are so much higher than our ways, and He so desperately wants us to walk in His ways. Regardless of what has been done to us, we have an opportunity to permit Him to change us in the midst of walking in the personal pain of adversity, hurt, and heartache. The author of Hebrews makes it very clear to us in the words quoted earlier:

> See to it that no one misses the grace of God and that no bitter root grows up to cause trouble and defile many. (12:15)

The most wonderful news I can give you is the glorious good news of Jesus Christ our Lord. At any point along this process of making choices—choices that result in a downward spiral away from the grace of God and into bitterness—there is grace and mercy from God available to us to take charge of our life and to change. I may choose His ways of love, mercy, grace, and forgiveness because He has made these available to me at the cross of Jesus. Let's take the sling of faith and head out into the valley of the heart to attack this internal giant of bitterness. Let's stop at the brook on the way out and pick up our five smooth stones so we have projectiles for maximum impact on this giant of the heart.

Smooth Stone #1: The Word of God

The first stone we need to have available to sling at the giant of bitterness is what the Lord Jesus has given to us in His Word. As His people we are called to live in the provisions of Jesus Christ. By definition, we as His disciples do not assume our human ways nor our rights, but we choose to follow the ways of Jesus. Speaking to each one of us, Jesus says, "Deny yourself, take up your cross and follow me" (Matt. 16:24).

As previously stated, Paul tells us to embrace the attitude of Christ Jesus. The Lord has given us very clear words about the fact that we have been given complete forgiveness of sins and our offenses to God by His grace. We could do nothing to gain our forgiveness. We were totally dependent upon the Lord Jesus to give it to us. What we have been so freely given, we're commanded to freely give! The Word of God says we don't have to live with growing resentment and bitterness. We can forgive our offender and the offense as an act of grace, whether they ask or not. We are responsible for taking the Word by faith as a weapon and applying it to the places of the heart in which the enemy is capable of working. So let's take the following scriptures as personal words of God Almighty to believe, receive, and proclaim against the inner giant of bitterness:

> For if you forgive men when they sin against you, your heavenly Father will also forgive you. But if you do not forgive men their sins, your Father will not forgive your sins. (Matt. 6:14–15)

> Do not let any unwholesome talk come out of your mouths, but only what is helpful for building others up according to their needs, that it may benefit those who

listen. And do not grieve the Holy Spirit of God, with whom you were sealed for the day of redemption. Get rid of all bitterness, rage and anger, brawling and slander, along with every form of malice. Be kind and compassionate to one another, forgiving each other, just as in Christ God forgave you. (Eph. 4:29–32)

Bear with each other and forgive whatever grievances you may have against one another. Forgive as the Lord forgave you. (Col. 3:13)

Smooth Stone #2: Brokenness of Heart

The second stone we need to take and place in our shepherd's bag is the choice to be broken in heart by the hurt, wound, or offense that has been done to us. The Lord has permitted it to happen to us, so we need to choose to ask Him to speak through it to us. We need to let brokenness run its course and do what God has in mind to do with this season of the heart. We need to take the time to allow ourselves to see what this wound has exposed to us that the Lord wants us to see. The Lord has precious lessons for His children that we can learn only in the school of the broken heart. Wounds can be used by God to show us areas of our lives in which we are not trusting the Lord with surrender. Trusting Him deeply is a precious thing to the Lord. It is so important to Him

> **We need to let brokenness run its course and do what God has in mind to do with this season of the heart.**

that we have noticed He will either have us voluntarily embrace brokenness or He will force it upon us as His sons and daughters. He is more concerned about our learning to walk in the image of His Son Jesus than our comfort. He says in Isaiah 57:15:

> For this is what the high and lofty One says—he who lives forever, whose name is holy: "I live in a high and holy place, but also with him who is contrite and lowly in spirit, to revive the spirit of the lowly and to revive the heart of the contrite."

Smooth Stone #3: Confession of Our Need

When we have thrown brokenness of our heart at this internal giant, the next logical step is to confess our need of His provisions of grace, mercy, and forgiveness for our offender and their offense against us. The Lord delights in this humble response of His people who have chosen not to take their own rights to be hurt and offended victims. He delights in His sons and daughters who will admit they don't have what it takes to forgive and release their offenders from resentment and bitterness. To pour out in confession to God the offense we have carried, and the fact that we have been on the downward spiral away from grace and into bitterness, is very special to the Lord. To admit we don't have what it takes and can't do this for ourselves is a sweet-smelling offering to the Lord. The issue of confession is really important to the Lord, because we are expressing our faith and surrender to Him.

Smooth Stone #4: Coming Near to Him at the Cross

The fourth stone we need to have in our shepherd's bag is what we earlier saw James describe for us in James 4:8:

"Come near to God and he will come near to you." We noted in chapter 3 that when we draw near to Jesus at the cross and lay in His bosom offenses that have been done to us, He literally bears them away from us. He destroys their power over us by taking them into Himself and crucifying them for us. In the awesome "unfair exchange," He takes into Himself my sinfulness as all well as the sins done to me with their wounding and heartaches, and He gives me in return His provisions of righteousness, grace, and forgiveness.

The power of bitterness is rooted in the offense and the feelings surrounding it. When the Lord takes the offense into Himself at the cross and destroys it we are set free to experience the awesome freedom of releasing and forgiving our offender for Jesus sake. When the giant of bitterness is slain in our hearts at the cross and His powerful provisions of forgiveness and grace are taken by faith and confessed against it, there's a huge inner *thud!* There's another shorter giant!

Smooth Stone #5: Being Filled with the Spirit

The final stone to take against the giant of bitterness is asking the Holy Spirit of the risen Christ to come into our hearts and stand up strong in the place where the offenses against us once stood. The Lord Jesus promised us another Counselor to be with us and live in us. He taught us that just as a dad loves to give good gifts to his children, so the Father is delighted to give His Holy Spirit to us those who but ask. The key here is that, after we've gotten out our wounds at the cross, we need to invite Him to fill us with His heart and mind for our offender. What a marvelous joy to have the powerful, living Jesus Christ in our hearts, moving us to walk in His ways. He gives us victory over the fallen giant of bitterness. What a joy to be able to remember the hurt and offense and not feel ill inside. What a blessing to see the offender and have the powerful presence of the living Christ release love and compassion through us to them!

As we wrap up this chapter on the inner giant of bitterness being overcome by the provisions of Christ Jesus our Lord, let me encourage you. If you have an inner debt of the heart, a wound that has never been adequately addressed at the cross, the seeds of bitterness probably reside in that wound. If you give the enemy an inch in your heart he will invariably work to expand it. Child of God, don't be fooled. Don't put up with anything you know to be contrary to the will of God. Bitterness isn't something you have to learn to live with and seek to control. You can get rid of that inner giant of the heart that stands in the valley yelling at you, "You can't beat me!" To do so, you will have to be as ruthless with this giant of the heart as it has been in seeking to imprison you in its grip. Get your sling of faith and go throw some stones. Go after the internal enemy and do some giant-slaying!

Chapter Nine

Defeating the Giant of Guilt

AS WE TACKLE OUR NEXT giant of the heart, I just want to remind you that you are an overcomer. You can walk into the valleys of the heart with the kind of faith in Christ that produces courage, optimism, and confidence. Please remember, He has given you His precious promises and His Spirit to guide you and cheer you on. The Lord takes great delight in those of us who choose to be His without reserve and who walk with Him in deep confidence that He will do what He has said He will do. Second Chronicles 16:9*b* says,

> For the eyes of the Lord range throughout the earth to strengthen those whose hearts are fully devoted to him.

Paul adds a word for us in the second letter to the Corinthians that, in essence, says that all of the promises God ever gave to us in Scripture are "Yes" in Christ. Through our prayer lives the "amen" that is proclaimed to the glory of God the Father (see 2 Cor. 1:20). As we attack internal giants of the heart, it is important that we first fix our eyes on Jesus, our victorious Warrior and then look at the giant-sized obstacles that stand in the way of a more intimate walk with God.

Armed with an attitude of faith in the majestic Lord God, the truth of His Word, and a heart of deep submission to Him who loves us intensely, let's attack our second giant of the heart: *guilt.* When I use the word *guilt,* I am referring to the inner sense that I have committed an offense against a known value, moral issue, or law. It is an inner negative feeling of having failed, of having sinned against God. The Lord God wired us, as His creation, with the ability to feel guilt so that we could learn to know His will and walk with Him in obedience. Feelings of guilt, though negative for a time, are actually a good creation of God, an act of His grace. These feelings lead us to own our offense or sin, to be broken by our failure, and to confess it to God so we may find forgiveness from Him. He affords us the opportunity to walk in cleansing of sins and failures through the precious blood of Jesus Christ, shed for us on the cross. When we appropriate these provisions of grace and forgiveness by faith, He removes our guilt from us and places in us His gift of righteousness in Christ.

In our culture here in North America, we have seemingly decided to turn away from biblical truth. We have embraced a value that we should not receive the inner message of guilt. Today we believe if it is a negative feeling or sense, it must be bad and should be avoided at all costs.

Recently I was reading a number of quips taken from a Christian periodical that illustrate the point:

- In 1980 a Boston court acquitted Michael Tindall of flying illegal drugs into the United States. Tindall's attorneys argued that he was a victim of "action addict syndrome," an emotional disorder that makes a person crave dangerous, thrilling situations. Tindall was not a drug dealer but really was a victim of thrill seeking.
- An Oregon man who tried to kill his ex-wife was acquitted on the grounds that he suffered from "depression-suicide syndrome"—a disorder whose victims deliberately committed poorly planned crimes with the unconscious goal of being caught or killed. He didn't really want to shoot his wife; he wanted the police to shoot him.
- Then there's the famous "Twinkie syndrome." Attorneys for Dan White, who murdered San Francisco Mayor George Moscone, blamed the crime on the emotional stress linked to White's junk-food binges. White was acquitted of murder and convicted on a lesser charge of manslaughter.

The common thread in all of the above is that, though having perpetrated some terrible crime, none was found guilty. They were victims! Today, in our culture, it's as if nobody is guilty of anything. We just do not accept personal responsibility for the choices we make, because if we did, the next step would be to accept guilt, which is not acceptable to us. Guilt is, by definition, a negative feeling and therefore is considered reprehensible. We refuse delivery and so are forced to find ways of rationalizing away our wrongs, or worse, finding someone else or something about our culture or heritage to blame for what we have done.

The capacity to feel guilt is from the Lord God our Creator. He has made a way to deal with and remove guilt that results from acts of sin and wrongs we have committed. Salvation history is the story of God's reaching and redeeming love. It reveals His heart of mercy and kindness, taking to Himself and crucifying our sins so we might be cleansed of them. The Lord removes all that we stand guilty of before Him if we will own our wrong or sin, confess it, and repent of it. The love of God for us finds its highest expression in Jesus, the Son of God, shedding His blood for our cleansing and forgiveness of both sins and the guilt we feel because of them.

The Inner Giant of False Guilt

One of the enemy's most crippling weapons—one he has used on the people of God for centuries—is heaping on us feelings of condemnation. The enemy seeks to have us feel condemned in heart over something we have owned and for which we have repented and that the Lord Jesus has cleansed by His grace and mercy. Feelings of condemnation can result in our walking around in the inner bondage of false guilt—an unhealthy guilt that can and does rob God's people of life, hope, and joy. Condemnation from false guilt can arise from one of two sources in Christians:

First, condemnation can arise from a nagging sense that what I have done is somehow too big for God to forgive and cleanse from my heart. It is, at its root, a sense of not having appropriated the truth of the Word of God deeply in our heart by faith. It is choosing to go on living as if we are not forgiven, not being able to forgive ourselves for what we have done. God has made it very clear concerning His desire to forgive and willingness to do so when we genuinely ask in faith.

> Therefore there is now no condemnation for those who are in Christ Jesus. (Rom. 8:1)

Second, feelings of condemnation arise from the evil one's tempting and seducing spirits, who entice Christians to feel a nagging sense of free-floating guilt that is just always with them—the sense that "this seems to work for everybody but me." There is no legal right for this free-floating guilt, no real reason for it to exist in the heart. It is just there by enemy design. Throughout Scripture we are told that the enemy is the author of slander, accusation, and condemnation against the believers. The fruit of condemnation is always negative emotions that destroy hope and resolve in the people of God to fight the good fight of the faith and lay hold of eternal life.

One of the enemy's most crippling weapons . . . is heaping on us feelings of condemnation.

Here's a truth regarding false guilt and the enemy's condemnation. We are actually participating in a lie of the enemy, a lie that says what the Lord Jesus Christ has done is insufficient to set us free from the sins from which we have repented. The result of accepting this lie in our hearts is that we live under a dark cloud of negative emotions and oppression. We literally believe there is something wrong with us that the Lord hasn't or can't fix. The result is that there are unpaid debts affixed to our soul by our own choices!

Here's a second truth regarding false guilt for sins and wrongs we have committed and for which we have repented at the cross. This is always the work of the enemy designed to remove the hope of Christ from the believer's life. Sometimes condemnation remains in us because we are familiar with and have grown accustomed to negative emotions and feelings about our walk with God. Some Christians were raised in a legalistic environment of constant fire-and-brimstone preaching that used guilt pressures as a motivation to get right with God. As a result of living with that kind of teaching in their heart for a decade or two, some of God's special sons and daughters actually believe they can't be pleasing to God if they have positive feelings about their walk with the Lord. They erroneously conclude that it is prideful to feel good about themselves and their walk with God by faith. Therefore, it is more spiritual—and ultimately more familiar—to embrace negative feelings about myself.

Here's a third truth we need to know about false guilt and condemnation. No matter how many times we repent of these feelings, they never go away. No matter how broken we are by them or how many times we confess and repent, the feelings never leave. Actually they expand, leading the child of God down a road of deeper cycles of negative emotions. Healthy guilt leads to a broken heart, godly sorrow, and repentance. When we embrace these steps healthy—that is, Spirit-inspired—guilt is removed from us.

On the other hand, the inner giant of false guilt from the enemy actually expands with brokenness, confession, and repentance. It stands in the valleys of the heart and mocks us, "You can't beat me!" False guilt can only be defeated by declaring the falsehood of it and claiming the truth of God against it.

Dealing with false guilt isn't about an issue that causes guilt, it is about feelings of guilt that have no basis. What matters is what God has said that He has done for us in Christ Jesus our Lord! What defeats this inner giant of false guilt is the destruction of the lie we have believed. This is done through confessing it, renouncing it, and embracing the truth of Jesus that sets

> **. . . the inner giant of false guilt from the enemy actually expands with brokenness, confession, and repentance.**

us free from the lies of the enemy. Let the smooth stone of the Word of God whistle through the air, propelled by the sling of faith, and strike this giant of false guilt in the forehead, destroying it.

The Giant of Personal Guilt Before God

To really get at this issue of the inner giant of personal guilt, it needs to be said that acting like we don't feel it or finding temporary relief from it is definitely not the same thing as dealing with it and having it removed from our lives. To refuse delivery from guilt or taking medication to feel better about ourselves will only mask the inner issues of the heart. To keep on turning away from personal responsibility, finding someone else to blame for what we have done wrong, will not remove it. The fact is that what we have done wrong broke an inner law of the heart, transgressing our conscience. There are always two people who are well aware that the inner giant of personal guilt is standing in our hearts, taunting us. We know we feel guilty for what we have done, and God knows we are guilty before Him. Attempting to deal with these deep feelings in a light manner will not get at what really needs to be done for our good.

If we look at the words of Jesus to His disciples in the upper room, He helps us to really come to grips with this whole issue of personal guilt before the Lord. He spoke about the Holy Spirit of God coming to us as an inner Counselor and initiating healthy guilt within each one of us on a personal level. He does this initiation of guilt in us so that we may experience ownership of what we have done wrong, confession of sin, and repentance of our ways. He longs to give us the deep joy and wonder of experiencing His forgiveness, which has powerful cleansing effects. The only way we can experience this sweet love and mercy is to come to grips with ourselves and our ways in the light of His glory and His ways.

> When [the Holy Spirit] comes, He will convict the world of guilt in regard to sin, and righteousness and judgment: in regard to sin, because men do not believe in me; in regard to righteousness, because I am going to the Father, where you can see me no longer; and in regard to judgment because the prince of this world stands condemned. (John 16:8–11)

On the evening of His death, as He spoke to His closest followers, He shared a body of truth with them from which we can draw applications to our own lives. He pointed to the fact that after He had shed His blood for us on the cross and had been risen from the dead, He would send the Holy Spirit to live within us and convict us of sin before the Father. Feelings of guilt—the nagging sense of negative emotions felt in the heart—are in fact, a messenger of grace. Far from turning away from these and choosing not to embrace them, the Lord desires that we feel the guilt and allow His Spirit to draw us to the cross to deal with the sin causing the guilt. Jesus promised His followers that they would experience conviction of guilt in three ways:

1. We will feel guilt for sins we have committed that make us guilty before God, who is absolutely holy. These sins must be dealt with by faith, and cleansed and forgiven by Him.
2. We will feel guilt due to righteousness we do not have and cannot produce by our own efforts. We must be given His righteousness by His grace, only in and through the crucified and risen Lord Jesus. (The Lord Jesus was trying to help His people to see that self-righteousness is no righteousness at all.)
3. We will experience guilt in regard to judgment God will exercise, regarding how we have lived, because God is holy and just.

We must experience judgment in one of two ways. We can choose to judge ourselves sinners now in this life and thereby experience the mercy and grace of Jesus Christ our Lord, who takes the penalty of judgment for our sins on the cross. Or we can wait until this life is over and stand before the judgment seat of God Almighty and be judged a sinner when it is too late to change. Jesus used a word-picture, the meaning of which is hard to escape. Just as surely as Satan, the "prince of this world" now stands condemned even though it hasn't happened yet, even so sin must be judged!

If we are going to face and defeat this internal giant of personal guilt before God and our own conscience, we are going to have to grab the sling of faith and the smooth stones the Lord has given to us as holy projectiles to destroy guilt. The good news in the Scriptures is that the Lord has already defeated guilt for us, and our job is to merely appropriate by faith what Jesus has done.

Smooth Stone #1: The Word of God

The first stone we place in our shepherd's bag as we march out into the valleys of the heart to face this inner giant of guilt is what God has said to us regarding the destruction of guilt through the provisions of Christ Jesus. The Word of the Lord is really clear about the issue of His removing our guilt. The Father placed our guilt for sins we have done in our Lord Jesus Christ as He offered Himself for us on the cross. What we must do is to take this provision of the Word of God and attack the inner giant of personal guilt by faith, proclaiming the death of guilt in Jesus Christ our Lord. Here are but three such promises to be taken, believed, and claimed:

> God made him who had no sin to be sin for us, so that in him we might become the righteousness of God. (2 Cor. 5:21)

How much more, then, will the blood of Christ, who through the eternal Spirit offered himself unblemished to God, cleanse our consciences from acts that lead to death, so that we may serve the living God! For this reason Christ is the mediator of a new covenant, that those who are called may receive the promised eternal inheritance—now that he has died as a ransom to set them free from the sins committed under the first covenant. (Heb. 9:14–15)

If we confess our sins, he is faithful and just and will forgive us our sins and purify us from all unrighteousness. (1 John 1:9)

Smooth Stone #2: Brokenness of Heart

The second stone to place in our shepherd's bag as we march out to attack the giant of guilt is allowing guilt to have its effect of breaking our heart. This is the central thing the Lord is after in His sons and daughters, because it is one of the sacrifices in which He delights.

The sacrifices of God are a broken spirit, a broken and contrite heart, O God, you will not despise. (Ps. 51:17)

We need to allow guilt to deliver its message and deeply embrace the brokenness for our sins. We need to let brokenness run its course so that we can see not only what we've done that is displeasing to God, but also have the Spirit of God as our Counselor teach us what is in our hearts that motivated us to do it in the first place!

Smooth Stone #3: Confession of Our Need

As we have embraced a broken heart because we have felt the healthy, Spirit-motivated guilt, we need to move on to confession of what He has permitted us to see in our hearts that caused the guilt. God communicates to us, over and over in the Word, that He absolutely delights in a humble response of confessing our needs to Him. The humble person who cries out to God for what he or she can't produce by human grit and determination will always be met with warm acceptance at the throne of grace. Guilt is destroyed, as the reason for its existence is admitted and repented of as specifically as we can. We feel guilt over sins we have committed. We lack righteousness and have omitted doing His will at times. We face His judgment for what is in us that shouldn't be there.

Smooth Stone #4: Coming Near to Him at the Cross

We have noted several times that the Book of James teaches us, "Come near to God and he will come near to you." When we draw near to Jesus at the cross, and lay in His bosom there the things for which we feel guilty, He takes them and bears them away from us. In so doing, He destroys our personal guilt. He actually becomes guilty for us as He takes our sins into Himself and crucifies them for us. We have described this as the "unfair exchange" in which God makes Jesus, who knew no sin, to become our sins, and then He gives us Jesus' righteousness as a gift of grace. The power of guilt is rooted in offenses. The Lord destroys its power by removing the offense, while giving us the incredible gifts of release and forgiveness of sins.

Smooth Stone #5: Being Filled with the Spirit

The final stone to take in this defeat of the inner giant of guilt is to invite the Holy Spirit to dwell in our hearts and live where the offense and guilt once stood. What a marvelous joy to have the risen Christ Jesus standing in us, in person, at the very places where we have felt guilt for sin and in our areas of unrighteousness. What a place of victory of the heart for the sons and daughters of God. The Spirit witnesses to our spirit that we are God's sons and daughters. He makes the mercy of God a personal and living reality in our hearts.

As we wrap up this chapter on the issue of personal guilt initiated by the Lord in our conscience let me encourage you to accept the message guilt seeks to send. The only way it remains as a giant of the heart is if we operate as though it doesn't exist, try to give it time so it will go away, or try to find something or someone else to blame for what we did. How much better to accept personal responsibility for the offense and get on with destroying guilt through brokenness of heart, confession of our need, drawing near to Jesus at the cross, and inviting the Spirit to dwell in us in power! We don't have to learn to live with this thing. Let's do some holy stone throwing!

Chapter Ten

Defeating the Giant
of Loneliness

THINK WITH ME ABOUT this precious issue of walking in spiritual victory today in and through the provisions of Jesus Christ our Lord. We are enabled by the indwelling Holy Spirit of the living God to live as more than conquerors—to reign in life. The apostle Paul wrote one of my favorite verses in Romans 5:17:

> For if by the trespass of the one man, death reigned through the one man, how much more will those who receive God's *abundant provisions of grace* and of the gift of righteousness *reign in life through* the one man *Jesus Christ.* (emphasis mine)

Paul encouraged the believers in Rome, and in turn, you and me, to walk in the provisions of grace that are ours in Jesus Christ our Lord. We are not called to live this life as those who just "get by" or who "hang on by the skin of our teeth." We are called to walk by faith in who He is and what He has promised He will do. We are called to choose to take the Word of God as a weapon, to believe it, and to proclaim it as truth that sets us free from the inner giants of the heart.

Armed with this truth and accompanied by an attitude of a warrior of God, let's march out into the valleys of the heart and address our third giant: *loneliness*. This giant-sized obstacle to walking in God's ways fills the human heart with a sense of being all alone. It can be described as an internal, nagging ache of the heart, a longing to know and to be known—that is, to share a meaningful relationship with another. As a pastor, I watch people very closely. I have watched people come to our church with maybe five hundred other people in the building and yet feel desperately alone. I have been at a shopping center and have seen lonely people go to a checkout counter and buy an unneeded item just to talk to the person behind the counter.

My perspective may be a bit biased, but I honestly believe the culture in which I live here in North America is a society of lonely and disconnected people. In our culture it is as if many of us have signed our own personal "declaration of independence." Furthermore, we are reaping the fruit of decades of secular humanistic teaching that places "me" at the center of the world. Our worldview, or the lenses through which we view life, are built around the question "How does it impact me and mine?" We are a culture full of desperately lonely people who have espoused and lived two values that are detrimental to the human heart:

1. *Rugged individualism,* which is in essence, telling myself and others some or all of the following: "I

don't need anybody's help"; "I can make it on my own"; "No one is going to tell me what to do"; "I am the judge of what's best for me." The problem with rugged individualism is that it just doesn't work, because we are all wired with an inner need to know and to be known. We all desire fellowship. John Donne wrote, "No man is an Island." Another problem with rugged individualism is that we all have a real problem being objective with ourselves. We tend to remember things with our own bent, or selectively, at best. Consequently, we don't really see ourselves wholly until we can see ourselves through the lenses of others.

> **We are a society of people who . . . go through life with a nagging sense inside of the need to be meaningfully touched by another person.**

2. *Isolated living,* which we have espoused in this upwardly mobile culture. Let's go get the most money and the best package of perks, regardless of how far removed we are from family and those who really know and love us. Look at our homes: We arrive at 6:00 P.M. to live behind our green, chemically treated

143

moat-and-hedges; we can "eat in"—even have "eating out" delivered to our doorstep in thirty minutes or-less or the next one's free; entertainment is readily available within the confines of our home; we don't have three generations living on the same farm anymore—probably not even in the same state; we don't even choose to get to know our neighbors. We're alone and isolated night after night.

The upshot of all that I am saying here is that we have embraced these values and now we are living with the fruit thereof: loneliness. We are a society of people who smile empty smiles, look at each other with hollow eyes, and go through life with a nagging sense inside of the need to be meaningfully touched by another person.

The Society of the Lonely Hearts

For many, many people who live in our culture today, there is a deep sense of inner debt. There is an almost guilty feeling of the heart that we are all alone in life, that nobody knows us well, and maybe worse, nobody cares. This inner sense of longing can actually produce a kind of free-floating guilt that people struggle to put a finger on. This can come from an inner condemnation of the heart lonely people often feel when they ask and wrongly answer the question: "Why am I so alone?" The conclusion they arrive at is, "There must be something wrong with me. No one seems to want to get close to me or stay close to me."

Feelings of loneliness and free-floating guilt—perhaps more realistically described as self-condemnation—can be absolutely overwhelming at times. Self-condemnation speaks the inner message of the heart that there really is something wrong with me. Yet there's nothing on which to hang the inner accusation, except that nobody really knows me or seems to want to know me deeply. These intense feelings of loneliness can actually bombard a person while standing in a room full of people. Feelings of loneliness can and often do flood a husband and wife who may be struggling to meaningfully relate to one another. They can be in the same bed and yet feel miles apart emotionally.

Personally, I believe loneliness is one of the reasons the corner bar is so well attended and why bartenders are known as people who have listening ears. The hit television show *Cheers* was on for many seasons because it was so relevant to where so many people live today. The creators of the series made a long run of shows that humorously portrayed people who were lonely misfits in various real-life situations. The theme song even talked about being at a place "where everybody knows your name and they are always glad you came." Millions watched this show about a corner bar and were fascinated by it because it clearly touched their hearts.

We are definitely the society of the lonely hearts. Feelings of profound loneliness spring from the lack of fulfillment of an inner desire the Lord God, our benevolent Creator, wired into all of us. There is one major factor, among others, that separates us from the rest of the animals on earth. We are made with the need for deep, intimate relationships that are personal and permanent. We literally crave fellowship—to know and to be known well. There's a verse of Scripture relative to this that I just can't escape:

The Lord God said, "It is not good for man to be alone. I will make a helper suitable for him." (Gen. 2:18)

In that context, relationship had to do with permanent, heterosexual monogamy. It included marriage to one life-long partner of the opposite sex—a soul mate and friend with whom to procreate. But we are also shown in Scripture people in same-gender, deeply intimate friendships and mentoring relationships that also get at this human need to know and to be known. One such scripture that comes to mind is the relationship between Jonathan and David:

> So Jonathan made a covenant with the house of David, saying, "May the Lord call David's enemies to account." And Jonathan had David reaffirm his oath out of love for him, because he loved him as he loved himself. (1 Sam. 20:16–17)

These two men made a covenant with each other to be brothers to each other, no matter what. There is a powerful relational need being met in their lives through this friendship.

In 2 Samuel 1:26 David is lamenting the death of his very best friend, Jonathan, on the battlefield. His heart cries out in anguish as he grieves the loss of his deep and intimate friendship with his brother-in-law.

> I grieve for you, Jonathan my brother, you were very dear to me. Your love for me was wonderful, more wonderful than that of a woman.

Those words have absolutely nothing to do with sexual expression. It is a testimony of David's sense of loss of an intimate friendship, which he realized was not something to be taken for granted. The verse describes what it really means to have a same-gender person in whom you can confide and with whom you are comfortable relating. There is an inner satisfaction that comes from knowing someone—a satisfaction that sexual expression cannot touch. Sexual desires are only satisfied for a short time, then return powerfully. This friendship David had with Jonathan was more profound than something fleshly. God made us relational beings, therefore feelings of loneliness are so very difficult for us to endure. We need to know and be known.

> **We are made with the need for deep, intimate relationships that are personal and permanent.**

When loneliness has gripped the human heart, it is sometimes a result of a person's lot in life—being alone through no fault or choice of their own. Having to relocate to another part of the country to get a job in our field can do this to us. Or family tragedies, death of a loved one, or death of a marriage can put us in a place of loneliness. But more often, I believe, it is a result of choices people make as a result of hurts and hard experiences in relationships. These hurts and heartaches can have lasting and permanent debilitating effects if we allow them.

The choice to go it alone is often made as a result of feelings of pain, hurt, and heartache over broken relationships. We very often give in to feelings of personal guilt over perceived failures and inadequacy. Then, in a sort of encyclical spiral downward toward loneliness through self-condemnation, we give way to fear of failure or being rejected again. We perceive the potential pain of further rejection to be too great and, with or without evidence, draw the conclusion, "I just couldn't bear to be hurt again. I will not risk openness again." We fold up shop and decide the pain of loneliness is less than the pain of being hurt again.

The Lord Jesus came to earth to show us the need we all have of loving and being loved by God. This is the big thing loneliness misses out on: *love.* It is the necessary ingredient to what Jesus talked about as the two greatest things we can experience in the kingdom of God—loving God and loving people. When we decide to go it alone, we often shut out God and God's people. We miss the wonder and the joy of loving and being loved by God. And we miss the joy of loving and being loved by His people. As Christians, this is totally unacceptable. In fact, it is sin. Jesus taught us that the measure of our love for God and for people is how we know we are in His kingdom of the heart. Loneliness is an inner giant that has to be faced and defeated, children of God. So, hey, grab your sling of faith, and let's walk over to the brook together to pick out our five smooth stones!

Smooth Stone #1: The Word of God

There are many scriptures to which we could turn at this point to see this whole issue of our need to know and to be known. We have already alluded to a number of them in this chapter. The concept I want to raise here, however, is that we will not really be enabled to seek to know others until we have first dealt with our inner compulsion of the heart to know our Father God through Jesus Christ our Lord. The truth of the Word is that when we have come to know Christ as our Lord and Savior, we are never alone again. On the eve of His death, the Lord Jesus gave us some absolutely tremendous promises we can read in the Book of John:

> The world cannot accept him, because it neither sees him nor knows him. But you know him, for he lives with you and will be in you. I will not leave you as orphans: I will come to you. Before long, the world will not see me anymore, but you will see me. Because I live, you also will live. On that day you will realize that I am in my Father, and you are in me, and I am in you. Whoever has my commands and obeys them, he is the one who loves me. He who loves me will be loved by my Father, and I too will love him and show myself to him. (14:17–21)

> Jesus replied, "If anyone loves me, he will obey my teaching. My Father will love him and we will come to him and make our home with him. He who does not love me will not obey my teaching. These words you hear are not my own; they belong to the Father who sent me. All this I have spoken while still with you. But the Counselor, the Holy Spirit, whom the Father will send in my name, will teach you all things and will remind you of everything I have said to you. Peace I leave with you; my peace I give you." (14:23–27a)

There awaits, for everyone who desires to know the Father God through Jesus Christ the Lord, a deepening walk with God through life, by faith. He has made a way for us to deal with what keeps us from knowing Him: our sins and iniquities. He has destroyed these for us in His body, sacrificed as a redemption price for us on the cross. God loves us deeply and longs to know us so much that He became one of us to purchase our salvation, that we may walk with Him. The choice is absolutely ours because He has made a way for us to come to Him by faith. This is the first smooth stone we need to throw at the inner giant of loneliness: a walk with the Lord as Friend who sticks closer than a brother. Once we have by faith entered into knowing Him, He relentlessly draws us to His heart. The author of the Book of Hebrews said,

> Keep yourselves free from the love of money and be content with what you have, because God has said I will never leave you; never will I forsake you. (Heb. 13:5)

David one of our giant-slayers of Scripture wrote about a deepening, intimate walk with God in a powerful verse many of us have memorized:

> Because the Lord is my shepherd I shall lack nothing. He makes me lie down in green pastures, He leads me beside quiet waters, He restores my soul. He guides me in paths of righteousness for his name's sake. Even though I walk through the valley of the shadow of death I will fear no evil for you are with me. (Ps. 23:1–4)

Smooth Stone #2: Brokenness of Heart

Remember this is something that is very precious to God. When we are willing to bow before His throne of grace, embracing a broken heart before Him for our part in our own processes of pain, God the Father delights in us. "A broken and contrite heart, O God, you will not despise" (see Ps. 51:17). Our need is to permit our feelings of loneliness to bring deep and heartfelt brokenness to us. We're broken by our participation in dealing with the past hurt and rejection, with fear of being hurt again, and by making the choice of the will to turn away from people who would love us.

We need to be broken in heart by our will issues of deciding to feel the pain of loneliness rather than taking the risk of opening ourselves up to someone who could potentially hurt us. This fear is rooted in self-preservation and self-defense. When we are choosing to walk in these inner provisions we can give ourselves, we are not walking in trust and surrender to God as our shield and defender.

A broken heart before God chooses to trust in Him and surrender to Him even though we are brought to the place of needing to embrace heartache. My desire is to know and walk with God, and His desire is for my best and fullest maturation. He brings me messages about myself—things I couldn't see from my own limited perspective—through others. He works for His best in me and uses others in my refinement processes.

Smooth Stone #3: Confession of Our Need

We must move beyond the issue of embracing the message our loneliness is sending to us. We need to confess the stuff we are seeing and feeling inside so the enemy no longer holds us prisoners behind iron bars of the heart. The inner giant of loneliness is a giant of our own heart that we have allowed to live there. It can and must be defeated by taking down our self-defending masks and confessing our need of a deeply personal relationship with both the Lord and His people. What a freeing and liberating thing to embrace our weaknesses and inability to provide for our needs, confess them, and open ourselves to believing the Word of God in the process. Scripture is very clear that loving God more intimately will place in us the ability to enter into right relationships with others. This is part of our confession of our need. We need to confess that we can't make it on our own or live in isolation, that we do in fact need people to love and who will love us:

> Two are better than one, because they have a good return for their work. If one falls down, his friend can help him up. But pity the man who falls down and has no one to help him up! Also, if two lie down together, they will keep warm. But how can one keep warm alone? Though one may be overpowered, two can defend themselves. A cord of three strands is not quickly broken. (Eccles. 4:9–12)

Smooth Stone #4: Drawing Near to Him at the Cross

We have seen the fact that brokenness of heart and confession of our need are necessary parts to the process of healing. Yet the most important issue regarding our inner healing of life's giant-sized wounds is the biblical truth of drawing near to Jesus Christ our Lord at the cross and laying in His bosom, by faith, that which has imprisoned us. The truth of the Word of God is that God the Father meets with us there. By the powerful presence of His Holy Spirit He takes out of us what has imprisoned us and gives to us the righteousness of His Son Jesus. He destroys for all of us the barriers to deeper fellowship with Him and His people. Every one of us can and will experience His resurrection victory over this inner giant of the heart if we will humbly bow at the cross and have Him crucify our self-defending, self-preserving ways of loneliness.

Smooth Stone #5: The Fresh Filling of the Holy Spirit

The fifth stone to throw at the inner giant of loneliness is to invite the Spirit of God to come into your heart and fill you full of His presence. What a profound joy it is to sense the inner counsel and friendship of God because His Spirit is bearing witness with your spirit that you are a special son or daughter of God. This is the promise of God for all of us who believe. Yes, even to you!

Caleb, one of our other biblical giant-slayers, told his lifetime partner in spiritual battle, Joshua, that he could drive out the giants. Caleb told Joshua why he knew he could take care of the giants around Hebron. Caleb testified to the presence of God in his life and members of his family. Together with God and others he could do it! How about you? Do you face and defeat giant-sized obstacles and problems because you have the Lord and some key people in your life? Loneliness doesn't have to stay a part of our lives. Is that the whistling of a sling-born smooth stone projectile I hear?

Chapter Eleven

Defeating the Giant of Fear

A S PRESENT-DAY GIANT-SLAYERS we have been using the Old Testament giant-slayers, such as David and Caleb, as models for taking actions born of faith. The thing that is so wonderfully impressive about those Old Testament giant-slayers is that they were convinced of spiritual realities their physical eyes could not see. Ultimately, it is the spiritual battle that dictates the outcome of our physical circumstances.

David and Caleb were carried along by attitudes of courage and confidence in God's ability to take care of them regardless of the size of the obstacles that stood in their way. They were convinced the real issue of concern wasn't the giant that opposed them, or actions the giants were taking. They believed the real issue was the perfect will of God, what was He about to do? They knew they couldn't defeat their giant-sized problem by themselves, but by His strength and power they would win. They were so convinced of this fact that they actually guaranteed victory on the way to the battle! The Lord God smiled on them and honored their faith, giving them incredible victories.

Armed with similar hearts to know and please God and attitudes created in us by faith, we are called to face and defeat the giant-sized obstacles and problems facing us today. The presence of these giant-sized obstacles in our lives generally is an attempt by the enemy to get us focused on our circumstances rather than on the Lord. The giants we are looking at are those that live in our hearts. Some of these are external first, then impose themselves on us when we permit them to enter our thoughts and hearts. Some of them are internal giants we impose on ourselves. But all are equally malevolent and desire to destroy faith and confidence in God.

In this chapter we are facing our fourth internal giant of the heart we impose on ourselves: *fear*. As we begin this subject I want to remind you that the ability to feel and have fear is not bad in and of itself. Fear is a creation of God, imbedded in our humanity. It is meant to be a protective safety device for us. When we feel fear, we become more attuned to our circumstances, our senses are put on edge, our heart rate increases, and we take a defensive posture. Essentially, fear is a good thing. The root word in Old English means "sudden danger." It refers to fright that is justifiable, a danger that is concrete and knowable. In this sense, fear is appropriate because we are warned by it and can be kept from personal harm.

However, the internal giant of fear we are addressing in this chapter is more an internal anxiety of heart, a feeling of tightness in our chest. This sense of fear comes from within and remains in us even when there are no discernible stimuli to cause it to be there. This fear is that of the unknown; it is the what-if syndrome of life. It is an inner anticipation of pending doom that sends the internal message, "Something bad is about to happen, I just know it."

This internal giant is often hard to defeat because it is accompanied by so many other things, that can and do plague us as human beings. It lives with traveling companions, such as discouragement, suspicion and falsehood. Fears for which we can't pinpoint any cause can often be traced back to old wounds of the heart, debts created in us by others, or unmet needs we experienced. These old, unresolved issues can be a real

> **This fear is that of the unknown; it is the what-if syndrome of life.**

breeding ground for our enemy to sow lies that bring about irrational fears and anxieties within.

It is really important that we understand the aim of the enemy Satan, in these unhealthy fears, is to keep us inactive and unproductive in our faith-walk with God. The enemy will seek to paralyze our desire to take actions born of faith, even though we may be quite sure of God's will. Satan has been using paralysis as a tactic for thousands of years, and he's gotten pretty good at it by sheer repetition. His tactic is much like that of a lion that seeks to paralyze its prey with fear by its intense roar. The lion's aim is to get the prey to react or run away a bit slower to give the lion the advantage. In fact, Peter used that metaphor in his letter to believers:

> Be self-controlled and alert. Your enemy the devil prowls around like a roaring lion looking for someone to devour. (1 Pet. 5:8)

The enemy's goal is to get our eyes off of Christ Jesus our Victorious Warrior Lamb. He attempts to con us into believing that his ability to shatter our faith is more powerful than Jesus' ability to faithfully protect us. The devil's bluff is to get us to move a little further from the Good Shepherd; it's the old divide-and-conquer plan. He wants you and me to believe we are powerless against his wiles so we might just as well give up.

> . . . the aim of the enemy Satan, in these unhealthy fears, is to keep us inactive and unproductive in our faith-walk with God.

The truth we must remember is who we are because of whose we are! We belong to God the Father as His adopted sons and daughters, because we have been to Calvary by faith. We have experienced the cleansing of sins and have been given the Holy Spirit of God to dwell in our hearts. We have had the enemy's power over us destroyed in Christ Jesus and have become partakers of His kingdom of the heart:

> For he has rescued us from the dominion of darkness and brought us into the kingdom of the Son he loves, in whom we have redemption, the forgiveness of sins. (Col. 1:13–14)

158

The Son of God purchased us for Himself to be spiritual temples in whom the Holy Spirit of God Almighty dwells. In Christ, we have been granted victory over Satan and his miserable schemes:

> [Jesus] replied, "I saw Satan fall like lightning from heaven. I have given you authority to trample on snakes and scorpions and to overcome all the power of the enemy; nothing will harm you. However, do not rejoice that the spirits submit to you, but rejoice that your names are written in heaven." (Luke 10:18–20)

> You, dear children, are from God and have overcome them, because the one who is in you is greater than the one who is in the world. (1 John 4:4)

Our job is to stand firm in the faith He has given to us. We are to take and claim the victory of Christ Jesus our Lord and not be rendered paralyzed by irrational fears! The enemy uses lies, deceit, and our old wounds to create fears. His choice weapon is fear of inadequacy and fear of failure. This miserable internal giant of the heart bellows internal condemnation to us that sounds something like this: "Who do you think you are? What if you do attempt something for God and you fail miserably?" When we sense the nudge of the Spirit, let's choose faith in the mighty Lord God. Let's take His truth to defeat both the enemy and the weapon of fear.

Fear of Failure and of the Unknown: Gideon

One Bible story that comes to mind when we think of unhealthy, paralyzing fear—dread of the unknown and the potential of pending disaster—is the story of Gideon found in Judges 6 and 7. When we meet Gideon, he is threshing grain in a winepress while hiding in the hills in fear of the Midianite oppressors (see 6:12–26). He has surveyed the circumstances and has concluded the situation is hopeless. He can't possibly do anything about his Midianite oppressors, so he hides himself for fear of having stolen what little food he can provide for his family. One thing he has not done is ask God what He thinks about the Midianites and the apparent powerlessness and cowardice of Israel. He is operating solely on the basis of the internal message created by his human reason. He has embraced fear in his heart and has concluded it is hopeless!

I find it encouraging that the Lord didn't share Gideon's opinion of his circumstances. When God's angel came to him, he was told the truth of God and it overwhelmed him: "The Lord is with you, mighty warrior." From that point, Gideon was taken on a really remarkable adventure of faith that is just priceless to witness.

As you read through the story, God has him take small actions of faith and obedience to His ways and then rewards him tremendously for his willingness to walk with Him. God had him tear down his father's idols and told him to restore the sacrifices to Jehovah as the one true God. He led him on a journey to gather 32,000 soldiers to face possibly 100,000 of the enemy. Then, having mustered an army that is vastly outnumbered and underequipped for the battle, God gave him a series of tests for the soldiers, after which he had only 300 men left with him to go into battle.

All along the way, however, God built up this man's faith. He assured his man Gideon that if he fought God's way, trusting in the Lord for His power to save, he would see God's victory. The Lord had Gideon and his men march out with a trumpet with one hand and a clay pot with a lighted torch inside. He had them surround the Midianite camp in the night; shout to God; and break the pots, exposing the fire. Then they blew the trumpets from every direction around the camp. The Lord fought for them, and the Midianite army was destroyed. But perhaps more important to this study, Gideon had defeated paralyzing fear of the unknown in his own heart. He defeated fear of failure by trusting in and watching God come through on His promises. I'm personally convinced the Lord God was equally delighted with both victories—the one on the battlefield and the one in Gideon's heart!

Fearing What Is Seen in the Physical Realm

One outstanding scriptural example, of fearing what is seen in the physical realm, is the story of Simon Peter when Jesus came walking on the water to the disciples in the middle of the night. Lest we be too hard on Peter, I often ask myself the question *Would I have been in the boat with the guys who played it safe or on the water walking with Peter and Jesus?* Let's consider the story:

> During the fourth watch of the night Jesus went out to them, walking on the lake. When the disciples saw him walking on the lake, they were terrified, "It's a ghost," they said and cried out in fear. But Jesus immediately said to them: "Take courage! It is I. Don't be afraid." "Lord if it's you," Peter replied, "tell me to come to you on the water." "Come," he said. Then Peter got down out of the boat, walked on the water and came toward Jesus. *But when he saw the wind, he was afraid* and, beginning to sink cried out, "Lord, save me!" Immediately Jesus reached out his hand and caught him. "You of little

faith," he said, "why did you doubt?" And when they climbed into the boat, the wind died down. Then those who were in the boat worshiped him, saying, "Truly you are the Son of God." (Matt. 14:25–33, emphasis mine)

A second clear example of permitting the fear of what we can see to create a giant-sized problem inside is found in the Israelite army the day the teenage shepherd boy, giant-slayer David, showed up. In chapter 2, we focused on the way David heard the giant Goliath of Gath's words. He heard them through the filter of faith in an awesome and majestic Lord God Jehovah, whom he loved. David was in outrage at the defilement of the giant's words and the obscenities against the Lord's holiness. You know the rest of the story. But consider with me the fact that there was a large number of men who heard the same words every day. Yet they heard them through the grid of fear. They stayed behind the rocks and looked in fear at the giant who was so big he couldn't be defeated. Think about King Saul, who was himself the biggest male specimen in the army, and all of his soldiers who were supposedly the armies of God.

A champion named Goliath, who was from Gath, came out of the Philistine camp. He was over nine feet tall. He had a bronze helmet on his head and wore a coat of scale armor of bronze weighing five thousand shekels; on his legs he wore bronze greaves, and a bronze javelin was slung on his back. His spear shaft was like a weaver's rod, and its iron point weighed six hundred shekels. His shield bearer went ahead of him. Goliath stood and shouted to the ranks of Israel, "Why do you come out and line up for battle? Am I not a Philistine, and are you not servants of Saul? Choose a man and have him come down to me. If he is able to fight and kill me, we will become your subjects; but if I overcome him and kill him, you will become our subjects and serve us." Then the Philistine said, "This day I defy the ranks of Israel! Give me a man and let us fight each other." *On hearing the Philistine's words, Saul and all the Israelites were dismayed and terrified.* (1 Sam. 17:4–11, emphasis mine)

Look carefully at what is happening here. The giant has reduced the arena to the human plane. He has made it a contest between the Philistines and the servants of Saul. Because he has successfully done this he is able to create tremendous fear and dismay in Saul and all of his soldiers. They aren't there to fight for Saul. They are there to march into the battle for the Lord's majesty. The Lord who was with them and among them desired to be trusted and adored, and He Himself would have given these Philistines into their hands. Yet because their eyes were full of the giant, all of them—even the king—cowered in fear in the rocks and played it safe!

How adept the enemy is at getting us to focus all of our attention and activity primarily on the human and physical arena. Then we wonder why we live in fear and defeat. We haven't walked with God into the battles of life to see what His perspective is on the issues we are facing, let alone desired to do His will!

When David arrived on the scene he didn't stay on the human plane very long at all. It quickly became a contest between Goliath, whose power source was a block of stone named Dagon, and David who was empowered by God Almighty. The outcome was Jehovah 1, Dagon 0. Goliath, who served a block of stone, got stoned by a shepherd boy who loved God. For David, the really important issue was that the battle wasn't his at all. He knew the battle was the Lord's, and fear in his heart was destroyed by faith and courage.

> How adept the enemy is at getting us to focus all of our attention and activity primarily on the human and physical arena.

If you and I are going to walk out into the valleys of the heart to do spiritual battle against the enemy, we must do so with faith like David's. We attack and defeat the giant of fear by faith in God's provisions for us. Fear is merely the tool of the enemy which he uses to create paralysis in our hearts that we will not act in faith. We must learn to recognize irrational fear for what it is—merely a tool the enemy uses to keep us from trusting Jesus—and realize that it exists only when we allow it. So grab your sling and let's get the smooth stones we need from the brook.

Smooth Stone #1: The Word of God

Unhealthy fear must be attacked with the weapon of the Word of God. The Lord has made it clear to us that He is omnipotent and awesome God. He is a mighty fortress and a strong tower of defense around us. We need to grasp and be gripped by the power of God who lives in us by His Spirit. He makes His Word come alive in us by His anointing, and He teaches us to use it as a weapon when it is confessed through lips of faith. We can not permit the enemy to reduce the issues of life to the human arena or have our perspective limited by the size of the obstacles we face in life. Fear of failure or of the unknown is diminished when exposed to the truth of God:

> For you did not receive a spirit that makes you a slave again to fear, but you received a Spirit of sonship. And by him we cry, "Abba, Father." The Spirit himself testifies with our spirit that we are God's children. (Rom. 8:15–16)

> [Jesus said,] "I tell you the truth, anyone who has faith in me will do what I have been doing. He will do even greater things than these, because I am going to the Father. You may ask me for anything in my name and I will do it." (John 14:12–14)

> God is love. Whoever lives in love lives in God, and God in him. In this way, love is made complete among us so that we will have confidence on the day of judgment, because in this world we are like him. There is no fear in love. But perfect love drives out fear, because fear has to do with punishment. The one who fears is not made perfect in love. (1 John 4:16b–18)

Smooth Stone #2: Brokenness of Heart

Permit the message delivered by the unhealthy fear to have its way in breaking your heart. Brokenness is special to God. Choose to face the issues in your heart that your fear has permitted you to see, and be broken by your needs. Perhaps you will find old wounds in your heart in which fear has taken root. Permit the brokenness of your heart to draw you to seek Him in His majesty and holiness, and choose to look at yourself in the light of His love and grace.

Smooth Stone #3: Confessing Your Needs to Him

Choosing to face and admit fears and confessing them to God brings them out into the light of His love. The enemy works only in that which we permit to live in the darkness of our hearts and lives. When we reach out in faith and open ourselves to the Lord, He is delighted to come to our rescue! Openness to God is done through the choice we make to confess what we are permitting to live in us and by expressing our need for His power and majesty in our lives.

Smooth Stone #4: Drawing Near to Him at the Cross

As we bring the things to the cross of Jesus by faith and lay them in His bosom there, He crucifies and destroys our fears. He also destroys everything that is in us that offends the heart of God. All that has wounded us, as well as the things that can and do act as prisons of the heart, are destroyed as we bring them to the cross by faith and see them crucified with Him there. Irrational fears, unhealthy fears of the unknown, or fear of failure must be destroyed by Him if we expect to be victorious over them.

Smooth Stone #5: Being Filled Anew with His Spirit

He longs to fill us with His presence and walk with us by His Spirit. Jesus told us that all we need to do is ask Him, and the Father will give us the Holy Spirit to live in us. Jesus told us He would send another Counselor—the Spirit of Truth—who would live with us and be in our hearts. The Bible's promises relative to the filling of the Spirit are in the present, indicative tense. We are to go on being filled with the Spirit. When He lives in us, He doesn't permit fear to live with Him, He causes us to trust the Lord in everything. He is the very presence and the power of God in person in our hearts.

The giant of irrational and unhealthy fears can not stand where the Lord God reigns. We don't have to put up with the works of the enemy. We don't have to cave in to what once imprisoned us. We can walk into the valleys of the heart and attack and defeat the enemy, armed with the power of God, trusting in His Word! Don't permit any of the events of your yesterdays to defeat you today or tomorrow. The message of the grace of God is that we can start over again. We are more than conquerors through Him who loved us and gave Himself up for us. Cut the giant of fear down to size!

Chapter Twelve

C2

Defeating the Giant of Sin

A S WE THINK ABOUT attacking and defeating giants of the heart, it is important to remember the Lord Jesus desires us to walk with Him in spiritual victory in life. A very key principle for giant-slayers is that the first battlefield we are called to enter is the battlefield within. That's really the essence of this study: sons and daughters of God learning to face, attack, and defeat some rather imposing inner giants, and by God's power, experiencing victory over them. All too often these inner giants of the heart have stayed in us because we have either attacked them in our human strength, grit, and determination or we've assumed it's just the way we are and so we'll have to live with it. Both options are dead wrong. Anything in my life that is contrary to the will of God, as revealed in the Word of God, must be defeated, displaced, and destroyed. The only way that can happen is to take an approach similar to the one David took against Goliath. When the giant bellowed his obscenities at David, the shepherd boy's response was to honor the Lord God Jehovah:

> The battle is the Lord's and he will give you into our hands. Then all the world will know there is a God in Israel. (1 Sam. 17:48b)

We have chosen to believe God and face the internal giants of the heart. We are seeing God's will and His provisions of power to take us where grit and determination can't. We have watched them fall one by one as we have taken the Word of God by faith and have proclaimed His victory by His Holy Spirit's power.

We are armed with the Word of God as a weapon and attitudes of the heart to which faith gives birth: courage and optimism, regardless of the size of the obstacles before us. Walking in the fear and presence of God, permits us the joy of attacking inner giants from the perspective of His protection and grace.

> He who dwells in the shelter of the Most High will rest in the shadow of the Almighty. I will say of the Lord, "He is my refuge and my fortress, my God, in whom I trust." Surely he will save you from the fowler's snare and from the deadly pestilence. He will cover you with his feathers, and under his wings you will find refuge; his faithfulness will be your shield and your rampart. . . . "Because he loves me," says the Lord, "I will rescue him; I will protect him, for he acknowledges my name. He will call upon me and I will answer him; I will be with him in trouble, I will deliver him and honor him. With long life will I satisfy him and show him my salvation." (Ps. 91:1–4, 14–16)

So let's take His provisions available to us in Christ and get after this next inner giant of the heart we impose on ourselves: *sin*. Sin can be defined as "wrongdoing, transgressing a moral law, offending or breaking the law of God." While there are no degrees of sins, or categories of greater and lesser ones, there are certainly varying degrees of depravity in human beings, dependent upon the willful choosing to commit sin. Scripture teaches us about sin in two different ways:

First, there are individual acts that are sinful. Such acts of sin occur when we know the right and do not do it, or when we do

> **The nature we choose to desire and feed in our hearts will live in control of us.**

what we know to be wrong, transgressing a known law. Choosing to go on sinning, or living in sin, results in separation from God, because holiness cannot have fellowship with willful, unrepentant sinfulness.

> Everyone who sins breaks the law; in fact, sin is lawlessness. (1 John 3:4)
>
> All wrongdoing is sin, and there is sin that does not lead to death. (1 John 5:17)
>
> Anyone, then, who knows the good he ought to do and doesn't do it, sins. (James 4:17)

But even more insidiously, there is in our humanity a sinful nature, a carnal or fleshly bent that seems to be drawn to sin repeatedly against God. Both sins and the sinful nature live our humanity. The sinful nature has been a part of being human ever since we chose to sin against God's desires in the Garden of Eden. Probably the most clear scripture regarding the character and existence of this giant of the heart—the fleshly nature—is what Paul wrote to the believers of Galatia in Galatians 5:17–21:

> For the sinful nature desires what is contrary to the Spirit, and the Spirit what is contrary to the sinful nature. They are in conflict with each other, so that you do not do what you want. But if you are led by the Spirit, you are not under law. The acts of the sinful nature are obvious: sexual immorality, impurity and debauchery; idolatry and witchcraft; hated, discord, jealousy, fits of rage, selfish ambition, dissensions, factions and envy; drunkenness, orgies, and the like. I warn you, as I did before that those who live like this will not inherit the kingdom of God.

Paul's words are really descriptive, aren't they? He speaks under the direction of the Holy Spirit and addresses a bent toward sinning that lives in our hearts as a part of our humanity. We have a built-in predisposition to turn away from walking with God and surrendering deeply to His will and ways. When we turn to Jesus Christ as Savior and Lord, inviting the Holy Spirit of God to take up residence in our lives there is an inner war begun, between the Spirit and the sinful desires. Our hearts truly become a battlefield for control of our direction and behavioral decisions. Paul went on in the next chapter of that same text to tell his readers a truth too many of God's people seemingly don't hear or perhaps don't understand. The nature we choose to desire and feed in our hearts will live in control of us. The nature we choose to starve will lose control of our lives. The issue of which nature reigns is subject to choices we make in our will, thanks be unto Jesus our Lord.

> Do not be deceived; God cannot be mocked. A man reaps what he sows. The one who sows to please his sinful nature, from that nature will reap destruction; the one who sows to please the Spirit, from the Spirit will reap eternal life. Let us not become weary in doing good, for at the proper time we will reap a harvest if we do not give up. (Gal. 6:7–9)

The Universal Nature of Sin in the Human Heart and Life

Another crucial issue found in the Word of God, regarding the presence of sin in the human existence, is the fact that sin is universal. Every person who has ever lived, or will ever live on this planet, has sinned and fallen woefully short of the glory of God. The only exception was Jesus, who was the sinless Son of God in human form. It is the common lot of humankind that we have sinned in thought, word, and deeds. We all have transgressed the will of God, and as a result of our choosing to sin, we are separated from fellowship with Him.

> Everyone has turned away, they have together become corrupt; there is no one who does good, not even one. (Ps. 53:3)

> Who can say, "I have kept my heart pure; I am clean and without sin"? (Prov. 20:9)

> We all, like sheep, have gone astray, each of us has turned to his own way; and the Lord has laid on him the iniquity of us all. (Isa. 53:6)

All of us have become like one who is unclean, and all
our righteous acts are like filthy rags; we all shrivel up
like a leaf, and like the wind our sins sweep us away.
(Isa. 64:6)

For all have sinned and fall short of the glory of God.
(Rom. 3:23)

If we claim to be without sin; we deceive ourselves and
the truth is not in us. (1 John 1:8)

Scripture is quite clear on this issue of the universality of
sin. Those who wrote the Scriptures, under the inspiration
of the Holy Spirit, seemingly didn't want us to be confused
about this issue. Sin is common to all of us. Because as human beings, we have a sinful nature that is bent on sinning,
all of us have committed sins. If we say we have not sinned,
we are deceived and subject to the evil one's lies.

The Different Ways Sin Dwells in Our Humanity

That we have all sinned is firmly established. The moti-
vations and the desires of our hearts to walk with God and
turn away from sinning against God are more subjective.
The really crucial issue—the one the Lord God seems to
bring under scrutiny regarding sins we commit—is what
we cherish in our hearts. What is going on in our hearts, or
our will, when we sin? The will to walk with God and turn
away from sin and sin's destructive path is very important
to Him. There is a difference in Scripture, between the in-
tending to commit sin and failing to achieve the purity we
desire. The one who doesn't want to sin, turns away from
it, and yet falls into it, has a heart to please God. The one
who desires to sin and intentionally goes about sinning,

has a heart to walk in sin. There is a great chasm of difference between these two kinds of hearts. The Scriptures also describe some different ways sin flows into and dwells in our lives.

First, Scripture discusses the issue of generational sin. What we are talking about here are patterns of sinful behaviors that are indigenous to certain family lines. One can see this in a family tree that has generational alcoholism or drug addiction that can be traced back several generations. Past generations of adulterous relationships may parallel a person's present-day struggle with lustful types of behaviors, such as the rush of feelings they receive from pornography. These sin strongholds can be broken at the cross of Jesus by the present family member who wants out. Freedom can come through ownership of and repentance from the generational sin. That is not to absolve the present practitioner of his or her guilt in the issue. Nor does this do anything to help someone's ancestors who lived with this issue. It is merely an attempt to explain the drawing—the almost irresistible nature—of a particular sin weakness that dwells in a person's heart and mind.

> The will to walk with God and turn away from sin and sin's destructive path is very important to Him.

Everyone is responsible for his or her own sinful actions. Everyone must come to Christ as an individual, repent of sin, and receive His merciful love, grace, and forgiveness personally. However, there can be patterns of weakness that get passed down to them, patterns that can be destroyed at the cross of Christ through the gift of "identificational repentance." This kind of repentance involves merely identifying with the family sin, owning it, repenting of it, and renouncing its hold on us, thus destroying its power to hold us in bondage, through the provisions of Jesus.

I have had the profound joy of walking with people I love to the cross and helping them dump off inner propensities to specific sins. I have watched men weep out gut-wrenching identificational repentances for generational pornography that had led them into sexual sins. I have watched people be delivered from such issues as generational alcoholism through identificational repentance at the altar with God and His people in prayer. When you love to help people and you see someone walk free for six months or a year from a sin that once held them, you make mental notes to yourself. I realize that the above is subjective to human experiences, but God's presence and power are my object!

Some of my friends and colleagues in ministry seem to have a theological problem with this concept of generational sins on two bases. One, they say it is an Old Testament teaching not found in the New Testament. And two, they say all such things are done away with at the cross of Christ at our experience of salvation: "If anyone is in Christ he is a new creation; the old has gone the new has come!" (2 Cor. 5:17). Let's just look at both arguments briefly for scriptural merit.

The concept of generational sins passing on is definitely found in the New Testament, but even if it were not, it isn't abolished by New Testament teachings as, say, are the sacrificial system, Aaronic priesthood, etc. To argue such an important point theologically from a position of the New Testament's silence, is not wise. But it is a New Testament concept. Jesus spoke of it in Matthew 23:31–36, as did Stephen in Acts 7:51–53.

The concept of all generational issues having been dealt with at the cross in the new birth seems to totally deny the difference between the position of our hearts before God and the condition of our hearts in our present experience with Him. Those of us who work with people in local churches know the incredible strain that living with specific weaknesses to specific sins can place on a child of God. Then our theological boxes—our human attempts to explain the ways of God—can and do cause people to take a position of denial. We tell them they don't have such issues or that it is already cared for at the cross. They know the weakness is in them so they force the issue underground. They just pretend it isn't there anymore. Personally, as a pastor, I would much rather have someone deal with their weaknesses and propensities than stuff them, pretending they don't exist.

The second way that sin dwells in the human heart and life is in the issue of besetting sins, or habitual sins people keep on committing. There are patterns of sins and weaknesses to specific sins that dwell in people's hearts. The person may be free of it for a week or even a month and think its been defeated, only to fall into the same sinful behavior again a month later. Besetting sins always have root causes that also need to be found, understood and destroyed. One of these root causes for a person's bondage to besetting sin may be generational sin weaknesses passed on to them. Another root cause may be a wound from their past. These will continue to surface and defeat the person unless they decide to get serious with the sin and the root cause of it that is in them.

A besetting sin could be something like the person who struggles with any kind of pastoral authority and is publicly critical of spiritual leaders in general. This is really an unwise course of action for anyone to take, and it should be dealt with sooner rather than later. It is always wrong to make up and spread gossip about people, including spiritual leaders. Not only should the sin of slander be addressed, but also the wounds of the heart that are in the person's past (probably from their father or another authority figure who hurt them in the past).

> There are patterns of sins and weaknesses to specific sins that dwell in people's hearts.

As another example of a besetting sin, consider the issue of habitual exaggeration—stretching the truth to make the story a little more interesting. Not only should the sin of lying be addressed but the person also should look for the reason why they have an inner need to impress others. There may be deep inner debts that enslave the person to the desire for acceptance and the acknowledgment of others.

A third way sin dwells in the human heart is through willfully choosing to sin. Willful sinning over time, renders the person enslaved to that sin. In light of the fact that God Himself came to earth to redeem us from sin at the sacrifice of His own life on the cross, it would follow that He is especially offended when willful sin dwells in us. This issue often is rooted in the person's choices to continuously feed the sinful nature—the fleshly desires—until these are in control of them. There are two passages of Scripture that come to mind regarding this issue of choices we make to willfully sin, and thereby offend God. One of these passages speaks to the issue of the danger of willful sin. The other speaks to the fact that the only way to get rid of it is to crucify it. The power of the sinful nature must be destroyed, and that happens as it is, by faith, crucified with Christ Jesus our Lord!

> **Willful sinning over time, renders the person enslaved to that sin.**

> If we deliberately keep on sinning after we have received the knowledge of the truth, no sacrifice for sins is left, but only a fearful expectation of judgment and of raging fire that will consume the enemies of God. Anyone who rejected the law of Moses died without mercy on the testimony of two or three witnesses. How much more severely do you think a man deserves to be punished who has trampled the Son of God under foot, who has treated as an unholy thing the blood of the covenant that sanctified him, and who has insulted the Spirit of grace? For we know him who said, "It is mine to avenge; I will repay," and again, "The Lord will judge his people." It is a dreadful thing to fall into the hands of the living God. (Heb. 10:26–31)

Paul wrote to the believers in Rome about destroying the sinful nature's desires at the cross of Jesus, pointing to their having been crucified by faith with Him and to the fact that His resurrection life and victory was dwelling in them. He drew the following conclusion in Romans 6:8–14:

> Now if we died with Christ, we believe that we will also live with him. For we know that since Christ was raised from the dead, he cannot die again; death no longer has mastery over him. The death he died, he died to sin once for all; but the life he lives, he lives to God. In the same way, count yourselves dead to sin but alive to God in Christ Jesus. Therefore do not let sin reign in your mortal body so that you obey its evil desires. Do not offer the parts of your body to sin, as instruments of wickedness, but rather offer yourselves to God, as those who have been brought from death to life; and offer the parts of your body to him as instruments of righteousness. For sin shall not be your master, because you are not under law, but under grace.

Let's walk into this huge battlefield of the heart and choose to face this inner giant of sin. The Scripture just quoted teaches us the fact that we are not the slaves of sin and sinful desires if we are truly the sons and daughters of God. We have been given the victory of Jesus Christ our Lord over the power of sin. Grab your sling of faith and let's walk over to the brook to choose our five smooth stones. Rather than playing defense against this giant of the heart, let's decide to go on the offensive, through confession and repentance at the cross of Jesus, by faith in Him!

Smooth Stone #1: The Word of God

Throughout the Word of God it is made clear that our Lord Jesus has become, for all of us who believe in Him, our sin bearer. John the Baptist prophesied of Jesus: "Be-

hold the Lamb of God who takes away the sin of the world"
(John 1:29). The Lord Jesus Christ came to this earth, taking a human body, specifically so that He could take unto
Himself all of our sins and their penalty, death. He did this
on the cross for us because we could not remove sin from
ourselves.

> God made him who had no sin to become sin for us, so
> that in him we might become the righteousness of God.
> (2 Cor. 5:21)

> He himself bore our sins in his body on the tree, so that
> we might die to sins and live for righteousness; by his
> wounds you have been healed. (1 Pet. 2:24)

God dealt ruthlessly with this giant of sin, pouring
His wrath out on the sin His Son Jesus became for us,
because this giant can't be tamed. Sin can't be managed
and the sinful nature can not be reformed. Sin must be
killed. God's method of destroying the power of sin and
the allure of the sinful nature is still the cross of His Son
Jesus. If God dealt that ruthlessly with sin for us, you and
I had better be ruthless with it as well. The way has been
made for sin to be destroyed, in both actions and desires
that live in us. Our part in this process of the destruction
of sin is the decision of our will. Will I turn to Him and
take His Word as personal to me?

Smooth Stone #2: Brokenness of Heart

The second stone to throw at this inner giant of sin is
to permit brokenness to deliver its message to me. Without question, the enemy wants us to think we aren't so
bad and sin isn't so bad. He'll try to get us at this place by

having us compare ourselves with others who are doing "worse sins" than we are. The issue of our pride and our desire to deal lightly with this giant will be exposed to us by the Spirit of the Lord at the cross of Jesus when we see the sin that is in His body—the guilt Jesus bears—isn't His; it is ours! The only righteous response to One who comes to take my filth and give me His righteousness is the response of brokenness.

Smooth Stone #3: Confession of Our Needs

What God is after is the end of ourselves in regard to this inner giant of sin. He wants us to get to the end of both extremes of our humanity: (1) of rationalizing it away; and (2) of living hopelessly with failure. What God is after is the honest, brokenhearted confession of our need. Jesus often spoke to honesty and openness in prayer as He instructed His disciples about the kind of prayer God honors. He pointed to the prayer of a sinful man who beat his breast, wouldn't even so much as look to heaven, and said, "God be merciful to me a sinner." (see Luke 18:13). The Lord is after the inner honesty of a heart that is tired of trying to make its own way and is ready to make a deep confession of need!

Smooth Stone #4: Drawing Near to Jesus at the Cross

At the cross of Jesus Christ our Lord, all sin is destroyed, including the sinful or fleshly nature's draw to sin. The Lord God laid in Him all of our sins, His wrath for our sinfulness, and the penalty of our sins, which is death. When we come to the cross of Jesus and mean business with Him there, God does a divine exchange for us. God the Father takes out of us the sins we have committed, owned, confessed, and of which we have repented by His Spirit, and

He places in us the righteousness of His Son Jesus. God has also provided for us the death of our sinful nature in His Son Jesus. He desires to have us, by faith, crucify the fleshly nature that leans toward sin and to destroy its power over us at the cross. The issue is the surrender of our will and the ownership of His will to live above willful sin! The power is God's. The variables lie with our decisions of the will!

Smooth Stone #5: The Fresh Filling of the Holy Spirit

When He takes out of us what is displeasing to Him and cleanses us of all sin, He desires to live within that freshly washed heart, making it His new sanctuary. He longs to fill us with His Holy Spirit. He merely awaits our desire and our request that He do so. He longs to walk through life with us in sweet fellowship restored through the unfair exchange at the cross. Let's go on being filled with His Spirit daily. Let's enjoy walking in His awesome presence within and powerful anointing to live above the allure of sin!

Did I just hear the *thud* of a furious and ruthless enemy, cut down to size by a present-day giant-slayer? Giants hitting the dust. I love it when a good plan comes together!

Chapter Thirteen

Defeating the Giant
of Appetites

WE HAVE BEEN STUDYING the concept of choosing the attitudes of a child of God, of faith giving birth to courage and optimism in the face of life's hardships. We've used the Old Testament giant-slayers, such as David and Caleb, as our models of faith in action. We have looked at their choosing to live a lifestyle of faith in an awesome God and His abilities to give them victory over their enemies. We have studied their choice regarding their attitudes of confidence in God even before the battle had begun. There are several things to remember here:

1. According to military strategies and human reasoning, these men chose to face what the people around them had verified were unconquerable foes. These men, according to the knowledge gained by the human senses, were out of their minds!

2. They chose to live by faith and to see their battles ahead of them as spiritual confrontations by the enemy to keep them from walking with God. Consequently they chose to put their trust in God's ability to deliver them, not in their human resources or their lack thereof.

3. They chose not to believe the giants' testimony about themselves. The "You can't beat me!" bragging prior to the battle wasn't accepted as fact by God's instruments of faith, regardless of the data that was before them.

4. They were mightily used by God in the midst of incredibly difficult battles of life. He was glorified in them and then through them.

We, very much like they, face problems and difficulties of life. Life is sometimes quite unfair to God's people. In order to face and defeat the adversity and hardship life throws at us, we need first to win the inner battles with the giants of the heart. We must learn the principles of spiritual victory within if we are to be more than conquerors in our world! That's the basic aim of this study.

In this section of the book, we are facing and defeating the inner giants we impose on ourselves. In this chapter, we're looking at the sixth, and final, self-imposed giant of the heart: *appetites*. First and foremost, we need to address the fact that appetites are God-created, natural hungers, longings, and desires.

Because we are human, we all have appetites for food, water, relationships, acceptance, success, and sexual expression. These are God-created and are therefore good. God said so Himself when He created us. He looked at us and said we were "very good." Food tastes great and lemonade is wonderful when it's 110 degrees outside. Sexual expression is delightful to both partners and is considered by God to be right and good when it is expressed in the confines of permanent monogamy. Successfully doing meaningful work that helps people can be extremely satisfying. Without appetites, life would be pretty bland. However, the enemy seduces us to feed and overfeed our human appetites, enticing us to permit them to run amok and clamor for satisfaction.

When the Appetites Enslave People

The problem with appetites is that they are only satisfied for relatively short periods of time. They begin to clamor for attention and satisfaction shortly after their last feeding. It is crucial that we understand that appetites must be kept in balance or they will ultimately enslave us. Appetites can become overwhelming cravings and desires which can and do rule over us. When appetites are in control of us life becomes an encyclical search for satisfaction. When we begin to operate from the "have-to's" we have ultimately chosen the road to travel which leads to the destination of addictions or compulsions. Our enemy Satan seems to be tremendously proficient at drawing people into enslavement in these two areas:

1. *Desires*—the longing for fulfillment, craving, moving beyond the point of having wants and normal, balanced human appetites to the point of needing to have the desires fulfilled. The implication here is that of intense yearning and longing, for the satisfaction of any of our human appetites.

2. *Satisfaction/gratification*—the fulfillment of the yearning of the appetite run amok. The satisfying of the physical longing. These are only attained in short bursts. They will arise again and demand more gratification, generally with more stimulus than satisfied them the last time. These appetites run amok are temporal, worldly, encyclical, and sensual.

We can tell when appetites have begun to run amok within us when our physical desires actually begin to rule over our intellect, our will, or in the case of the child of God, our spiritual desires born in us by the Holy Spirit. We can tell appetites have become sinful cravings when we think or say things like "I know I really shouldn't be doing this, but . . ." When it comes to appetites run amok, the irrationality of good, rational and intelligent people is really remarkable! The following statements are made by people who know better, want to do better, and yet cave in to that which they crave: "I know my doctor warned me not to eat certain foods because it's harmful to my health, but I like them and what he doesn't know won't hurt him" or "I know I shouldn't drink beverages containing alcohol, because alcohol destroys brain cells, but I do it to relax, loosen up, and feel more at ease around people."

> **Appetites can become overwhelming cravings and desires which can and do rule over us.**

Back in chapter 6 we studied the concept of the enemy's use of the giant of worldliness to enslave good people. We looked at the Scripture in 1 John that describes how we are called to "not love the world nor anything in the world." I want to go back to that Scripture with you and look at how the worldly system seizes on the God-created appetites. It creates, through sinful gratification of good desires, inner enslavement to the person. The worldly system around us entices us to gratify, in a sinful manner, the appetites and desires.

Do not love the world or anything in the world. If anyone loves the world, the love of the Father is not in him. For everything in the world—the cravings of sinful man, the lust of the eyes and the boasting of what he has and does—comes not from the Father but from the world. The world and its desires pass away, but the man who does the will of God lives forever. (1 John 2:15–17)

Permitted to get out of control, however, appetites become sinful cravings that are a cruel taskmaster to people.

Now *there's* an appropriate Scripture text for our culture in North America. John describes a people whose appetites have become cravings that have enslaved them. Under the Spirit's leadership he had his finger on the pulse of life as he wrote those words. He wrote about literally being ruled by the cravings of the physical body!

The apostle Paul also wrote numerous passages about this issue of allowing appetites to rule over the intellect, the will, or the Spirit's desires for the people of God. Like John, as quoted in the above scripture, Paul believed appetites in and of themselves were good when kept in balance. Permitted to get out of control, however, appetites become sinful cravings that are a cruel taskmaster to people. In his letter to the believers at Philippi, Paul wrote a very straight word about the appetites being enslaving. His point in this portion of the epistle is that we do have a choice in the matter of appetite suppression or satisfaction. To permit them to get out of control is to have made terrible choices.

> For as I have often told you before and now say again with tears, many live as enemies of the cross of Christ. Their destiny is destruction, their god is their stomach, and their glory is in their shame. Their mind is on earthly things. But our citizenship is in heaven. And we eagerly await a Savior from there, the Lord Jesus Christ. (Phil. 3:18–20)

Jesus Addressed Appetites in His Teachings

John 6 records Jesus' dialogue with a group of people who had their focus on the wrong things in life. He had, up to this point in John's narrative, performed miraculous signs and wonders and had attracted a rather substantial following. Jesus was trying to teach the people, and show them by example, that satisfaction of the human appetites was not something they should be focused on at all. The human appetites must be kept in balance or they'll enslave people. The point of walking with God by faith is that our focus and desire must be to know Him, to walk with Him in relationship, and to seek to do His will for our lives. That desire in our hearts will keep all other appetites in submission. He presented the truth to them rather bluntly in this context. Listen to His words:

> I tell you the truth, you are looking for me, not because you saw miraculous signs but because you ate the loaves and had your fill. Do not work for food that spoils, but for food that endures to eternal life, which the Son of Man will give you. On him God the Father has placed his seal of approval. (John 6:26–27)

He clearly dealt with the issue of competing appetites in people. He was teaching a group of people

Jesus taught His people . . . that keeping appetites for the stuff of this world suppressed and under control is a matter of having a higher desire.

who wanted two things from Him: (1) more free food; and (2) being spectators in the supernatural arena with nothing demanded from them. The sentiment was something like "Let's go hear the carpenter preach, and he'll feed us." Jesus lumped it all together in one sum when he said, "Do not work for food that spoils, but for food that endures to eternal life, which the Son of Man will give you." What a confrontational word of truth to them, and it wasn't received all that warmly.

Later in that same context, we are told that "many of his disciples turned back and no longer followed him" (John 6:66). The stuff of this life will literally consume us if it is permitted. In His parable of the sower, Jesus spoke to His listeners regarding the seeds sown in the thorny soil: "They are choked by life's worries, riches and pleasures and they do not mature" (Luke 8:14).

Jesus taught His people, regarding keeping our appetites in control in His Sermon on the Mount, which was, in essence, His Christian manifesto (see Matt. 6:25–34). The conclusion He drew for us there is that keeping appetites for the stuff of this world suppressed and under control is a matter of having a higher desire. Listen to the Spirit as He anoints Jesus' words found in verses 31–33:

> So do not worry, saying, "What shall we eat?" or "What shall we drink?" or "What shall we wear?" For the pagans run after all these things, and your heavenly Father knows that you need them. But seek first his kingdom and his righteousness, and all these things will be given you as well.

Appetites and Our Cultural Values

Jesus' words "Do not labor for food that spoils" are tremendously relevant, even prophetic, to our culture today. Let's briefly consider four appetites we, as God's people, seem to struggle keeping balanced. In typical "preacherly" fashion I have four words that begin with the letter *s* to share with you:

1. *Smorgasbords.* I've noticed, in my travels around the churches in North America, we don't need secular restaurant critics. There is usually a group of people around the church who can tell you where to go to be able to eat the most good food for the least amount of money. There is nothing wrong with owning a smorgasbord or with periodically going to dine at one. The problem is when we haven't been able to strike a balance regarding food or have ignored the plumb line that indicates where healthy eating ends and gluttony begins. I'm talking about exercising moderation so we don't eat ourselves into being overweight or invite high blood pressure and heart disease. One way we can tell our eating is out of balance is when we talk too often about food. If you're wondering about how your conversations stack up, ask a friend for feedback, someone who isn't afraid to be honest with you!

2. *Success.* There are people in our culture who are so consumed with attaining a standard of success that the rest of their lives are out of balance. We often call them workaholics. Externally imposed standards of success, the right workplace, career path, salary package, etc., can and often do lead us into a life of incredibly shallow relationship with the Lord and with significant people in our lives. Appetite for successfully accomplishing significant work in life is a good thing. The problem is when it's out of balance. We can become so driven and compelled by success that

we sacrifice loving relationships with our family and forfeit inner peace on the altar of career.

3. *Stuff.* There are folks in this North American culture who are absolutely consumed with getting and amassing money and material possessions, with acquiring the things culture tells us are the components of the "good life." Things such as the right house in the right neighborhood, the right "look" for our spouse and our kids, the right car, and all the right toys of life to play with. I recently saw a bumper sticker that read, "The guy who dies with the most toys wins." I have a better one. Mine would read, "The guy who dies with the most toys is dead." It is a wonderful thing to be able to provide a nice home and conveniences for our family. It is a better thing to love them deeply, investing quality time with them and enjoying them, for *that is the good life!*

4. *Sexual Expression.* This is an incredible appetite in the lives of people in our culture today. This one is responsible for a fair amount of moral decline in this nation. The appetite for sexual expression is healthy and holy when it is in the confines of "terminal monogamy"—one man with one woman, living under God's guidance for a lifetime. The desire for sexual expression that includes steamy videos or reading material brings lust and its perversion into something very good and holy. All too often this enters into our Christian homes and can lead to unrealistic demands on one's spouse, as well as untold hurts and heartache. Sexual expression very easily can become a compulsion, as anyone who has ever struggled with pornography can tell us. Our

sexual appetite can and does have addicting capabilities if not kept in balance and under control!

The bottom line I'm seeking to have us to understand is that this inner giant of appetite must be faced and defeated. It is capable of ruling us if, when seduced by the worldly enticements around us and the fleshly or sinful nature within us, we gratify it wrongly, feeding it and permitting it to grow. This inner giant of the heart will consume us if we permit it. To keep it in check, I make it a point to ask myself some honest personal questions, before God and others whom I respect, my goal being to gain honest feedback to ensure appetites are in balance.

1. I'll ask myself if I am excusing drives and compulsions within myself or if I have recently heard myself say, "I know I shouldn't do this, but . . ."
2. I'll ask myself, "What desires have I chosen to set my heart on during the last week? The last day? Have I chosen to desire the will of God in my life, or have I sought after appetite satisfaction? Have I thought about and invested in what is physical only, or have I put my efforts into what God alone can feed me by His Spirit?
3. On what have I set my affections: this world and its desires, or the will of God for my life?

If we are going to march out into the valleys of the heart and defeat the inner giant of appetites we are going to need a David-like attitude of an overcomer. We'll need our sling of faith and shepherd's bag. We need to stop by the brook on the way out to the battle and pick up our five smooth stones as faith's projectiles.

Smooth Stone #1: The Word of God

When the Lord Jesus was tempted to satisfy His appetite for food and drink in a manner that was displeasing to God, He quoted the Word of God as a weapon against the enemy. Listen to these powerful words:

> It is written, man does not live by bread alone but on every word that comes from the mouth of God. (Matt. 4:4)

The principle the Word teaches is that there is more to life than mere appetite satisfaction. Jesus said in Luke 12:15,

> Watch out! Be on your guard against all kinds of greed; a man's life does not consist in the abundance of his possessions.

The Word of God, confessed through lips of faith is powerful and effective because God Almighty stands behind it to perform every promise.

Smooth Stone #2: Brokenness of Heart

If you see that compulsions and a drivenness toward satisfying your appetites is getting out of control, allow God's Spirit to break your heart over it. God allows us to see these issues in our hearts precisely because He loves us far too much to allow us to stay the way we are. He brings us into season of brokenness to show us the precious nature of His provisions for us and the frailty of our own attempts to better our lives. Let brokenness have its way in your heart and embrace its message. Let's agree with Him that we have needs, and let's humble ourselves in His sight. Brokenness before Him is a doorway to change!

Smooth Stone #3: Confession of Our Needs

The Lord desires that we be truthful with Him from the heart. He desires that we open up to Him and speak out whatever we see in our hearts and lives that is bondage to appetite gratification. Regardless of what our need is, He isn't surprised by it at all. Humility of heart and life are precious to Him. He awaits our honest confession, because we have owned our needs and our helplessness to change ourselves by sheer will and determination.

Smooth Stone #4: Drawing Near to Him at the Cross

Seeing our need, owning it personally, and being broken by it are important parts of the inner washing and cleansing we all need. Coming to the cross of Jesus, by faith, and laying the sinful gratification of appetites into His bosom on the cross is extremely difficult to do. The inner giant of appetite hates the self-denial and the crucifixion of the self with Christ Jesus at the cross. It is extremely humbling to know that the things we have been doing—even as a son or daughter of the Father—are responsible for putting Jesus on the cross in our place. Yet God does the unfair exchange for us there. He takes out of our hearts the offensive things we confess, and He gives us the righteousness of Christ.

Smooth Stone #5: The Fresh Filling of the Spirit

The inner giant of appetites is dealt a deathblow by us when we surrender to the Spirit of God in our hearts by faith. The people in whom God's Spirit dwells experience profound changes relative to the desires of the heart. He moves us to know the Father's heart, to experience the manifest presence of Jesus, and to desire what God desires. The human appetites that clamor for attention will be subservient to the sons and daughters of God who choose to keep on being filled with the Holy Spirit daily. *It's a matter of having and embracing a higher set of hungers* than those of the physical arena!

God's method of spiritual victory in the hearts of His people is still a profound and living faith in the person and the works of Jesus Christ our Lord. Romans 5:17 is a death-blow to the inner giant of the appetites:

> For if by the trespass of the one man, death reigned through the one man, how much more will those who receive God's abundant provisions of grace and of the gift of righteousness reign in life through Jesus Christ.

Take the giant of appetites on by faith in Jesus Christ. If there is a constant struggle with one of the appetites, exercise a fast from it for forty days. Bring it under subjection to Christ's desire to bless you with spiritual authority and power over the physical! *Whiz, splat, thud.* Another giant hits the dust! The flower of freedom from the inner, self-imposed prison of sensuality blooms and grows in another child of God!

Part Four

Giants of the Heart Imposed on Us by People We Love

Chapter Fourteen

.☙

Defeating the Giant of Being Betrayed

LET'S BRIEFLY RETURN to the metaphor of our being people of God who choose to face the inner giants of the heart. We are studying how our actions must be dictated by our faith in the promises of God because we know the one who made the promises is faithful. We are using the actions that faith birthed in an eighty-year-old man named Caleb and a teenage shepherd boy named David as illustrations of the actions of faith we need to take with the Lord today. These two men went after what seemed to be, humanly speaking, undefeatable, giant-sized enemies of God. They faced their circumstances and problems with an attitude of optimism and courage, birthed in their hearts because they believed in God and what His Word taught them about His faithfulness and power for those who believe.

As people who face inner giants of the heart, we need to make similar attitudinal choices. We need to be people of faith, optimism, and courage, because we have been apprehended by the promises of God in whom we have believed. Faith will cause us to face and defeat these inner giants of the heart because it takes the Word of God seriously. Listen to some words about God's power to stand behind His Word, written by Paul:

> For no matter how many promises God has made, they are "Yes" in Christ. And so through him the "Amen" is spoken by us to the glory of God. Now it is God who makes both us and you stand firm in Christ. He anointed us, set his seal of ownership on us, and put his Spirit in our hearts as a deposit, guaranteeing what is to come. (2 Cor. 1:20–22)

> I pray also that the eyes of your heart may be enlightened in order that you may know the hope to which he has called you, the riches of his glorious inheritance in the saints, and his incomparably great power for us who believe. That power is like the working of his mighty strength which he exerted in Christ when he raised him from the dead and seated him at his right hand in the heavenly realms. (Eph. 1:18–20)

The Psalmist adds a word about the facing and defeating of the inner giants of the heart. These inner issues are destroyed when we learn to take the Word of God, by faith, and apply its healing power to our hearts and lives.

> Then they cried to the Lord in their trouble, and he saved them from their distress. *He sent forth his word and healed them;* he rescued them from the grave. Let them give thanks to the Lord for *his unfailing love and his wonderful deeds for men.* Let them sacrifice thank offerings and

tell of his works with songs of joy. (Ps. 107:19–22, emphasis mine)

Armed with the Word of the Lord who loves us and is faithful to us, and being encouraged by faith's attitudes of courage and optimism, let's attack our eleventh giant of the heart: feelings of having been *betrayed by a friend.* Almost all of us have walked in days of feeling sick in the pit of our stomach because we have had someone we really love turn on us and speak hurtful words to us or about us to others.

When you hear personal and confidential information about yourself from a person to whom you didn't talk, it really hurts.

When you have entrusted yourself to someone, you have made yourself vulnerable to them. When you really love and respect someone's overtures of friendship, you open up to them and share your innermost feelings. There is nothing quite like the feeling inside when your confidence in another person has been premature and is broken by them. When you hear personal and confidential information about yourself from a person to whom you didn't talk, it really hurts. Let's be clear here, that what we are talking about isn't gossip or hearsay that such-and-such might have happened. We are talking about verifiable betrayal by someone to whom we have deeply entrusted ourselves.

When hurt in this way, the tendency is to follow a cycle of self-defeating isolationism, which does nothing to bring about remedial action or to alleviate our feelings. The cycle goes something like this:

1. *We "hole up."* We decide it is better just to escape from being with people at all. We choose to withdraw from people we love and respect, because, who knows, it just might happen again. And then, of course, if he or she knows, who else did the person in whom I confided tell? The cycle of self-pity and isolation from people allows the enemy of our souls the room to make things a lot worse in our minds than the real issue about which we have holed up. Heartaches have a tendency to grow in our self-imposed times of silence.

2. *We "clam up."* We decide to talk to no one about it. This isolation from people who might be able to help us carry the load is normal and human but it certainly isn't the most healthy action to take. The fact is that when we carry our hurt alone, it expands over time, because we mull it over and ponder it. We think about the how-could-they-do-that-to-me questions, and we feel a growing anger inside. Isolation and self-protection fail at the point of our being willing to start reconciliatory conversations with the friend who has offended us.

3. *We eventually "blow up."* As mentioned earlier, seething feelings of anger must have a place to be vented if they are not dealt with constructively. They will eventually emerge at the least opportune times, and often with people who have nothing to do with the hurt. Just because our feelings of anger are stuffed

beneath the surface and we aren't dealing with them, definitely does not make them go away. When it comes to anger over inner hurts we've suffered, the adage "Out of sight out of mind" definitely doesn't cut it. Stuffed anger is a bit like a volcanic eruption. It finds the path of least resistance to the surface and blows!

Stuffed anger is a bit like a volcanic eruption. It finds the path of least resistance to the surface and blows!

David's Expression of a Heart That Has Felt Betrayal

I am so thankful for the fact that when David wrote Psalm 55, he was candid with us about how he felt when a friend had betrayed him. His words allow us to see how a man who loved God dealt with this incredibly hard issue. This is a psalm of deep, honest, and heartfelt prayer, written during a very low period in King David's life. I want to try to show you some things, from his description of his heartache, things that are pretty much universal for us as people who want to walk with God while we hurt. Let's walk down through what David reveals to us about what he was feeling:

1. *Troubled Thoughts.* Verses 2b–3a read, "My thoughts trouble me and I am distraught at the voice of the enemy, at the stares of the wicked." David wrote about

thoughts that took him toward feeling distraught within. He was in self-induced encyclical patterns of thinking that were extremely unhealthy. Can you relate to your thoughts being troubled? Have we found ourselves entering into these unhealthy inner cycles of thought patterns when someone we really love blindsides us or hurts us. I think we can easily find ourselves traveling around these mental ovals of hurt, frustration, anger and withdrawal, self-pity, introspection and self-condemnation.

2. *Suffering and Heartache.* In verses 3b–4a David says, ". . . For they bring down suffering upon me and revile me in anger. My heart is in anguish within me." David revealed a profound inner suffering, a heartsickness, to the Lord and to the readers of his psalm. Again, this is so relevant to us. Have you noticed the fact that when you have been hurt in your heart, you feel sick inside and food doesn't appeal to you, there's this emptiness and upset feeling in the stomach? Personally, I think emotional hurts are harder to deal with than physical ones because they're harder to get a handle on, since they are so deep and elusive. At times it can feel a bit like trying to nail Jell-O to the wall.

3. *Overwhelmed by terror and fear.* Verses 4b–5 further record David's struggle: "The terrors of death assail me. Fear and trembling have beset me; horror has overwhelmed me." Again he revealed what is common to human nature when we hurt inside. David talks about trembling in fear, about how we can feel overwhelmed inside by the fear of the unknown. Here he even talks about thinking the most depress-

ing kinds of thoughts: "the terror of death." Emotional wounding can expand and create fear even in the most courageous of people! Remember this guy David was a teenage giant-slayer for God! If he felt like this, isn't it reasonable to think perhaps some of the rest of us just might too?

4. *The desire to escape.* Then we read in verses 6–8, "I said, 'Oh, that I had the wings of a dove! I would fly away and be at rest—I would flee far away and stay in the desert; I would hurry to my place of shelter, far from the tempest and storm.'" Been there, done this? When you have been hurt through betrayal of your trust and confidence, you just want to get far away and hole up. You don't want to see anybody or talk to anybody. You feel shame and embarrassment. You want to go think about what's been done to you and contemplate steps you'll take.

There is just no question about it in my mind. David knew what it felt like to be betrayed by a friend. Listen to him tell us in his own words about the reason for this tremendous heartsickness he was feeling inside:

If an enemy were insulting me, I could endure it; if a foe were raising himself against me, I could hide from him. But it is you, a man like myself, my companion, my close friend, with whom I once enjoyed sweet fellowship as we walked with the throng at the house of God. . . . My companion attacks his friends; he violates his covenant. His speech is smooth as butter, yet war is in his heart; his words are more soothing than oil, yet they are drawn swords. (Ps. 55:12–14, 20–21)

Please notice with me David makes it very clear to us that his feelings are so powerful because of his love and respect for the one who wounded him so deeply. He talks about this offender with some incredible language of love and friendship. He calls him "my companion, my close friend, with whom I once enjoyed sweet fellowship." This is the reason for the depths of his heartache. He tells us plainly he could bear the pain much more easily if the hurt would have been caused by someone whom he considered to be one of his enemies. He might have expected it from enemies. What has made it so hard is that he loves this man so much. It is betrayal of trust and confidence and it is by a friend.

The Lord has taught me a number of lessons through the "school of hard knocks" and the following principle is one of the lessons He gave me: *The cost of loving people is that they will hurt you sometimes. We are known to be His by our love. Consequently, to stop loving people when we are hurt is never an option.*

A number of years back, the US Army began to use a term that really bothers me. When one of our own men was killed accidentally by one of our own bombs, bullets, or missiles it was termed "friendly fire." My resistance to the term is the pain the family of the victim must feel when they are informed by the military their child, spouse or parent died due to friendly fire.

My reason for bringing it up here is that I think there is a fair amount of friendly fire in the kingdom of God. The pain caused by feeling betrayal by a friend definitely qualifies as friendly fire, at least in my way of thinking. Using nice terminology for it or hiding behind our cultural value of democratic process does nothing to ease how much it hurts to love someone and feel hurt by their words. I have had to deal with some Christian friendly fire personally, and it isn't easy to handle. Being a pastor of a large church, I get to see a fair amount of wounds that are created by sins of the tongue. The family of God, of all the people in the world, shouldn't be wounding each other with our words. The church should be a safe place where people's confidences are kept and we pray for each other!

> **The family of God, of all the people in the world, shouldn't be wounding each other with our words.**

There isn't any healing found in merely feeling the feelings of having been betrayed. It is also true that telling others how we feel about what the other person did to me only expands the wounding to others and does nothing to promote our inner healing. As God's people we also reject holing up, claming up, and blowing up as options for the community of the forgiven. It is so important that we come back to the truth of the Word of the Lord. There He reveals His desire to raise up the life, mercy, and forgiveness of Jesus in us by the powerful presence of the Holy Spirit. So grab your sling of faith, and on the way into this inner valley of the heart, let's go over to the brook and get our smooth stones.

Smooth Stone #1: The Word of God

I want to take you back to the passage of King David's heart cry when he was betrayed by someone he loved and respected deeply. He wrote some scripture that encapsulates God's Word regarding what He desires to give us when we have felt betrayed. David decided to take God's invitation in the Word very seriously. He entered into deep and intimate prayer conversations with the Lord and based his petitions on the faithfulness and friendship of God Almighty. Notice that David stood on the very nature of God as he knew Him. David was convinced the Lord who had protected him and blessed him in the past was there for him now, even though he felt the crippling wounds of betrayal by a friend:

> But I call to God, and the Lord saves me. Evening, morning and noon I cry out in distress, and he hears my voice. He ransoms me unharmed from the battle waged against me, even though many oppose me. . . . Cast your cares on the Lord and he will sustain you; he will never let the righteous fall. But you, O God, will bring down the wicked into the pit of corruption; bloodthirsty and deceitful men will not live out half their days. But as for me, I trust in you. (Ps. 55:16–18, 22–23)

There's just no question about it. When your heart aches, you must have a place to go that is safe and a strength to lean on that is far beyond what you can provide for yourself. The Lord reveals Himself in Scripture as our shield and defender, a strong and high tower into whom the righteous may run and feel safe. I love what the Lord anointed David's son Solomon to write in Proverbs 18:24: "A man of many companions may come to ruin, but there is a friend that sticks closer than a brother."

Prayer conversations with the Lord Jesus, based solidly on His nature and promises revealed to us in Scripture, can have a tremendous stabilizing influence on us when we walk in the valleys of the heart and face the inner giant of betrayal! The Lord Jesus told His disciples on the eve of His betrayal and crucifixion that once He was risen from the dead, the Holy Spirit would come and live in them as their inner Counselor. You might feel alone on an emotional level, brother or sister, but according to the Word of God, the Lord dwells in your heart by His Spirit. The two of you can walk in this together.

Smooth Stone #2: Brokenness of Heart

While this might not be valued very highly in our culture, it is highly valued in the presence of God. When we allow ourselves to feel we've been wounded by a friend's betrayal of our confidence, the message of heartache will have a breaking effect on us. This is very precious to God, and when offered to Him as a sacrificial offering of love, it always finds approval and a warm embrace at the throne of God. If we've turned away from people and have chosen to hole up, clam up, and potentially blow up, we need to be broken, putting away our self-defending choices and trusting Him to be our defender. When I am broken in heart, I am choosing to embrace His ways for me and the lessons He may desire for me to learn in this experience. A broken and contrite heart renders me a teachable person as I kneel in His presence at the throne of grace.

Smooth Stone #3: Confession of Our Need

Embracing the message of the hurt we feel and permitting it to have its breaking effect on us is good. Getting on with confessing our feelings and our needs to the Lord is better. When David walked through the heartache of betrayal by a friend, he entered into a time of deep prayer and got it out to God. That prayer is recorded in Psalm 55. In it he poured out what had been done and how he felt about it. He poured out to God in prayer how much he had loved and respected the one who offended him. We need to confess what we are feeling to the Lord. We need to confess the debilitating effect betrayal has had on us. It is important to get this out so we don't sink into isolation and stop loving the people of God and entrusting ourselves to them. The "I-don't-need-anybody" mentality, of rugged individualism or isolationism, is definitely out of step with the values of God's kingdom of the heart. Confessing that we need to know and be known, to love and to be loved by people, is a wonderful part of the process of healing the wounds of the inner giant of betrayal.

Smooth Stone #4: Drawing Near to Jesus at the Cross

The inner giant of betrayal produces profound brokenness, which we need to own. We need to go on to confession of the heartache we feel as another step in the right direction of experiencing the healing mercy and grace of God. The next step in this process is to walk by faith to the cross of Jesus and envision ourselves laying in His bosom our friend who betrayed us along with the feelings of infirmity in our hearts. At the cross, we bow before Him and lay off on Him the broken relationship with our friend who hurt us and the wounds and the offense. He takes these away from us and crucifies them for us. He bears the wounds and the feelings away from us and offers us the joy of His love, mercy, and grace to forgive our offender as we have been forgiven. I am amazed at the simplistic beauty of the unfair exchange at the cross of Christ Jesus our Lord. I stand awestruck at how wonderfully freeing it is to deal with inner giants of the heart, there with Jesus, in spirit and in truth.

Smooth Stone #5: The Fresh Filling of the Holy Spirit

The final stone to throw at the inner giant of having been betrayed by a friend is to invite the Spirit of God to come into your heart and dwell in the place where the offense stood. The Lord God desires to dwell in us as a consuming fire of holy love. He desires to be our inner Counselor of the heart, to move us to make righteous decisions out of the context of deep healing grace and mercy He makes alive in us.

The Spirit of God will move us to go and talk to our brother or sister who has broken our confidence. As He does so, it will produce fruit in keeping with His kingdom of the heart. He is a Redeemer and He moves us to act in motives of reconciling love and redemption. God will move us to go sit with and converse with the friend who has offended us and has broken our confidence, and He will direct us in giving that person a "good piece of His mind." The Lord will give us His Words of reconciling love to share with our friend. Once we have hurled all five stones at this inner giant of a friend's betrayal, we are set free to walk in His holy ways:

> . . . those who live in accordance with the Spirit have their minds set on what the Spirit desires. . . . The mind of sinful man is death, but the mind controlled by the Spirit is life and peace, the sinful mind is hostile to God.
>
> . . . You, however are not controlled by the sinful nature but by the Spirit, if the Spirit lives in you. And if

anyone does not have the Spirit of Christ, he does not belong to Christ. (Rom. 8:5–9)

Was that sound, I just heard, the *thud* of another giant of the heart falling to the ground? Are you increasing in your confidence as you launch His truth at the inner giants of the heart?

Chapter Fifteen

⟨⟩

Defeating the Giant
of Unfair Criticism

THROUGH THIS STUDY, we have been using the word picture of the Old Testament giant-slayers. The Word of God is written to show us the ways of God, who He is, and what He has promised to do. Scripture gives us real-life stories of how men and women were challenged to know and walk with God regardless of their circumstances. In times of trouble, while most people cower in fear of giant-sized problems, there have been some people whose faith in God has remained strong regardless of external evidence for or against what God had told them.

Our six giant-slayers were such people. They believed God's Word to be true, that He is faithful to His people, and that He keeps His promises to those who love Him and seek to obey Him. David, the teenage shepherd boy, was a young man of faith. He was overwhelmed by zeal for God's kingdom and glory on the earth. Armed with a heart of love for God, faith in His goodness, and a sling and five smooth stones,

David walked out to face and defeat a gigantic killing machine named Goliath of Gath. David put the Lord's reputation on the line that day, and God used David as a vehicle to give His people a tremendous deliverance!

That's the kind of attitude we need to cultivate in our own heart by immersing ourselves in His Words of love and promise to us! If we are to live in spiritual victory over the giants of the heart today, we need to take His Word as truth regardless of the size of the problems or obstacles in our lives. The outcome of every spiritual battle I fight is utterly dependent upon whose I am. If I truly believe God's Word as truth, I'll choose to make a similar confession as David made on the way out to meet Goliath.

> I come against you in the name of the Lord Almighty, the God whose armies you have defied. This day the Lord will hand you over to me, and I'll strike you down and cut off your head. . . . [so that] the whole world will know there is a God in Israel. All those gathered here will know that it is not by sword or spear that the Lord saves; for the battle is the Lord's and he will give you into our hands. (1 Sam. 17:45–47)

Armed with such an attitude of faith-inspired courage let's attack and defeat our next giant of the heart: *unfair criticism*. Unfair criticism is something life sometimes throws at God's people; it can be hard on us emotionally and mentally and can cripple us. Hurtful words of "concrete innuendo" or unsubstantiated gossip are referred to in Scripture as the wicked, sinful, and fleshly act of slander.

Let's try to grasp the truth about being slandered and understand the concomitant feelings placed in us by such wounding words. To get at its root, we need to look behind

216

the words and the physical vehicle through whom they were spoken. We need to look at the spiritual realm to see the real author of unfair criticism, slanderous words, unsubstantiated rumors, and gossip—all things that can create profound illness in the body of Christ. What these sins of the tongue create are the diseases of suspicion and distrust. Whose work is it to create such things in the Christ's church?

In John 8:42–47, the Lord Jesus was being slandered by human instruments—the religious status quo who was threatened by His popularity with the people. Jesus' words, which I will quote below, came on the heels of accusations by the religious leaders that He was the illegitimate son of another man. His accusers were saying, in effect, that they knew Mary was pregnant with someone else's baby when Joseph married her! Jesus cut right to the chase, unmasking the supernatural beings behind what was playing out in the human arena:

> Jesus said to them, "If God were your Father, you would love me, for I came from God and now am here. I have not come on my own; but he sent me. Why is my language not clear to you? Because you are unable to hear what I say. You belong to your father, the devil, and you want to carry out your father's desire. He was a murderer from the beginning, not holding to the truth, for there is no truth in him. When he lies, he speaks his native language, for he is a liar and the father of lies. Yet because I tell the truth, you do not believe me! Can any of you prove me guilty of sin? If I am telling the truth, why don't you believe me? He who belongs to God hears what God says. The reason you do not hear it is that you do not belong to God."

The author of slander spoken against Jesus, was Satan himself. In the Book of Revelation, Satan is called "the accuser of the brothers who accuses them before our God day and night" (12:10b). Though the words come out of human lips, they are authored by the enemy and his vast army of evil tempters.

The word rendered "slander" in the Greek is *diabolous*, meaning "double-tongued," "fork-tongued," or "devil-tongued." One of the things about unfair criticism that just rips at my heart is that it often occurs via the informal gossip lines in the church. Think about the authorship of slander and the reality of its existence in Jesus' church—the church He purchased with His blood. It is disturbing to realize that in the one place on earth where people should find an environment of healing, love, and grace to change by the Spirit's power, too often they instead become wounded by unfair, unsubstantiated rumors, that are slanderous! Who, do you suppose, fuels gossip lines and encourages communication in the body that wounds God's people?

The thing that makes unfair criticism hard to deal with is that it is often *aimed at people's character and motives*. It is impossible to defend oneself in regard to motives and character. If you defend yourself, you're defensive, and if you say nothing, your silence assumes your guilt. It is a classic catch-22 situation.

From a scriptural perspective, we aren't called by God to find dirt in another person's life . . . let alone call someone on the phone and talk about it. If we are led by the Spirit to see something that is displeasing to God in another's life, we should understand the revelation as a call to intercession. The constraint of Christ's love directs us to the prayer closet, where we cry out to God for them until He sends us to them by mandate!

As strongly as I can, I encourage you to steer clear of the informal gossip lines that often are active in local churches. The next time the phone rings and the caller hands you "concrete innuendoes" about another believer, decide not to receive them. Here's a tip that I have found works pretty well in such situations. When you are told some juicy tidbit of gossip about someone, speak something positive about the person back to the caller. If the caller doesn't get the hint, you may have to take the more direct approach. Ask the caller to go into fervent intercession for the person.

> One of the things about unfair criticism that just rips at my heart is that it often occurs via the informal gossip lines in the church.

All too often this giant of unfair criticism is alive and well, going unchallenged in the local church. As God's people we need to remember what it feels like to be targeted by gossip. We need to go one step further and practice the Golden Rule: "So in everything, do unto others as you would have them do unto you" (Matt. 7:12).

Unfair Criticism and the Inner Person

Often people are walking around, even in their adult lives, with debts that were placed in their hearts many years ago.

Many people grew up in a home environment of unfair criticism and as a result have tremendous inner wounds and debts. The message they have received and believed is that "I just do not measure up, and I never will." The one place on earth devised by God our Father as a safe place for a child to learn of Him and His ways is in the family. Unfortunately, many people have grown up in homes where there was no love, no development of trust, and no positive encouragement to attempt to do new things. The message that wounded and fearful people often place on their children, both verbally and nonverbally, is "Don't try it, you might fail." Often children of such homes couldn't please their parents fully, even in small ways, no matter how hard they tried.

The people who grew up with perfectionist parents, also grew up in an environment of unfair criticism. Kids who grew up in such homes couldn't please their parents or attain the lofty standards set for them. No matter how hard they tried, the inherent message was that they just didn't cut it. No matter how well the child performed a given task, the bar was raised a bit higher, and there was never praise for the attainments the child did achieve. On top of the lack of praise, there often were angry verbal assaults about the child's inadequacies. Consider the following:

1. The perfectionist dad who just couldn't be pleased no matter how successful the child was at any given task. When there were failures—and most children fail periodically at some things they try—there was a barrage of unfair criticism and hypercritical unkind words. "How could you be so stupid? At times you are so good-for-nothing that I wonder how you could be my son? I wonder if you'll ever amount to

anything!" When such words are pounded over and over into the soul and mind of a child, he or she will eventually come to believe them and, unless there is deep inner healing, will spend a lifetime proving or trying to disprove those beliefs.

2. The perfectionist mother's house was always cleaned to the "immaculate perception." Her demands for good behavior were too much even for adults to live with, let alone small children. Harsh scolding for messes, name calling, and shaming for accidental spills, have created wounds. The labeling "You are so messy, such a sloppy person" and the unfair communication "you always," or "you never" has harsh judgment behind it. Children who experience such demands and judgment may struggle the rest of their lives trying to live down feelings of shame and inadequacy.

> **. . . deeply damaged emotions are carried around like unpacked luggage through the child's adult life.**

3. Or take, for example, the child with other siblings who have themselves been targets of unfair criticism. These siblings, living in an unhealthy, critical atmosphere, may seek to get even or to deflect heat from themselves by hurting their

brothers or sisters. There's a sort of beat-them-to-the-hurt mentality in such homes.

What this kind of home environment breeds on the emotional level in the child is deep sadness of heart. The wounds experienced at an early age are often carried well into the adult years or maybe even to the grave. This is the enemy's goal as he seeks to create inner prison cells of emotional bondage in people. People with deep inner wounds carry emotional pain, destruction of their sense of value, and death to their self-esteem. The enemy loves to use these wounds inflicted during childhood. His kingdom of darkness is drawn to pain, just as vultures are drawn to a dying animal. John 10:10 says it clearly: "The thief comes to steal, to kill and to destroy."

The emotional debts are incredibly deep in a person who has lived with this kind of dysfunctional family system. Through unfair criticism, these harsh and critical words create damage in a child's heart. The result is one or all of the following:

1. *Affliction of the soul.* These are deeply damaged emotions are carried around like unpacked luggage through the child's adult life. Such people believe that they are "damaged goods" and that people really can't love them just as they are. They are left with the inner hopelessness of image management, trying not to let anyone see the terrible person they believe they really are.

2. *Infirmities of the heart.* These involve emotions that are ill and lacking the ability to attain recovery without help. People who carry debts of unfair criticism don't know how to attain a healthy perspective about

themselves. The love of God the Father seems like a mirage in the desert of the heart to them. They never saw or felt familial love from an earthly dad so they don't know how to give it to others or receive it from God the Father.

3. *Oppression of the enemy.* The spiritual tempters go to work on those emotional wounds of the past to oppress the mind and heart of the afflicted one with hopelessness. Thoughts of inner failure lead to discouragement and ultimately full-blown depression when these wounds remain in the heart.

There's a spiritual principle about wounding that is common sense but often overlooked by the sons and daughters of God. Wounding of the heart is really a result of sins against us. No amount of sorrow and repentance will bring about life-change in a wounded heart. The truth of the matter is that *wounds, affliction, and infirmity do not lose their power through remorse and repentance. They are destroyed only through the healing grace and mercy of God.*

The Lord Jesus Experienced Unfair Criticism

Our Lord Jesus experienced all of the above when He came to earth to carry out His mission as our Redeemer and Healer. Because He experienced this in His own life, He is uniquely qualified to be our Savior and *the Way* to the Father. Listen to Isaiah's words— written some seven hundred years before Christ came—that prophesied Jesus' infirmity of soul, affliction, and the enemy's works of oppression:

> He was despised and rejected by men, a man of sorrows and acquainted with grief. . . . Surely he took up our

infirmities and carried our sorrows, yet we considered him stricken by God, smitten by him and afflicted. But he was pierced for our transgressions, he was crushed for our iniquities; the punishment that brought us peace was upon him and by his wounds we are healed. We all like sheep have gone astray, each one of us has turned to his own way; and the Lord has laid on him the iniquity of us all. . . . He was oppressed and afflicted yet he did not open his mouth. (Isa. 53:3–7a)

It is very interesting to me that some of Jesus' harshest criticism came from the religious leaders of His day. These men were, without question, threatened by His popularity with the people, the power of His teaching, and the purity of His life. In Matthew 13:53–58, there's a story recorded that illustrates this point clearly. Jesus had come to His hometown of Nazareth after working awesome miracles by the power of God. Those in the synagogue were amazed at Him and talked about His humble roots:

Isn't this the carpenter's son? . . . And they took offense at him. But Jesus said to them, "Only in his hometown and in his own house is a prophet without honor." And he did not do many miracles there because of their lack of faith.

Finally there are the words of false accusation, slander, and the unfair criticism that rained down on Jesus from the people who demanded His crucifixion.

Those who passed by hurled insults at him, shaking their heads and saying, "So! You who are going to destroy the temple and build it in three days, come down now from the cross and save yourself! He saved others but he can't save himself! Let this Christ, this king of Israel, come down now from the cross that we may see and believe." Those crucified with him also heaped insults on him. (Mark 15:29–32)

The author of the false accusations and slander that Jesus was enduring was Satan himself. The effect he desired was to wound Jesus so badly by those words that he would be side-tracked from seeking to glorify God—His central purpose of doing the Father's will perfectly to the very end! Jesus endured the cross, despising its shame, for one reason. He was there to reconcile unholy people, including you and me, to a holy God. He was there to make peace with God a reality we can experience by faith. Because Jesus endured the cross, wounded hearts are washed and healed today!

It's time to go grab your shepherd's sling of faith and head into the valley of the heart to face this inner giant named *unfair criticism*. To attack and defeat this giant that bellows, "You can't beat me!" we'll need some ammo from heaven. Let's go over to the brook, pick out our five, smooth-stone projectiles, and determine in our hearts to go have maximum impact on this inner giant.

Smooth Stone #1: The Word of God

There are several truths of the Word of God we are going to need to use against the inner lies of the enemy. The first one is that you and I are precious to God our Father as sons and daughters, made so through the spirit of adoption. There is a word in Isaiah 43:1–4 that is really precious, and the Spirit of God has made it personal to me:

This is what the Lord says—he who created you . . . ,
"Fear not for I have redeemed you: I have summoned

you by name: you are mine. When you pass through the waters, I will be with you. When you walk through the fire, you will not be burned . . . since you are precious in my sight . . . and because I love you.

The Lord has taken away your punishment, he has turned back your enemy. The Lord, the King of Israel, is with you; never again will you fear any harm. . . . The Lord your God is with you, he is mighty to save. He will take great delight in you, he will quiet you with his love, he will rejoice over you with singing. (Zeph. 3:15–17)

I can't speak for you but I know what those words mean to me. God is for me. Who can be against me? God loves us as our tender and merciful Father. He longs for us and delights in us as His sons and daughters. When we choose to take these truths by faith and embrace them, own them, and confess them, the healing mercy of God flows. The dichotomy created in us by the wounds of others must be laid alongside these words of love from the Word of God, which carry the opinion of the heavenly Father. On whose opinion will you choose to base your opinion of yourself? Who are you going to believe? Will you believe those who wounded you, or God Almighty?

Embracing this truth by faith and living like we believe it will enable us to place our life in His hands. The second biblical truth we must take by faith is that He is faithful to us regardless of how we feel or perceive ourselves. He loves us and we can trust Him to reveal Himself to us as our Shield and Defender. We can run into our Fortress and hide in Him, because our Fortress is everywhere. When we know we are His and that He lives in us, we live with the primary approval of God, not human opinions. We learn the joy and freedom of playing to an audience of one. I can take the words of Jesus and know the truth of them:

> Blessed are you when people insult you, persecute you and falsely say all kinds of evil against you because of me. Rejoice and be glad, because great is your reward in heaven, for in the same way they persecuted the prophets who were before you. (Matt. 5:11–12)

Smooth Stone #2: Brokenness of Heart

Allow the hurt of the unfair criticism or slanderous gossip to bring about deep brokenness of heart, which is highly esteemed in the kingdom of God. Brokenness permits us to see weaknesses in us for what they are, and having seen them, God enables us to deal with them, by faith in Christ. The passion of a true disciple of Jesus Christ is to be conformed by His Spirit into His image, to mature in His likeness by His power. Brokenness is a tool of God in that process!

Smooth Stone #3: Confession of Our Need

Embracing the message of critical words and being broken in heart by them are steps along the pathway to the deep healing of God's grace. It is important that we get these feelings out of our hearts, confessing our needs in prayer conversations with the Lord. It is important that we express to Him our need for His provisions. We need grace, mercy, and forgiveness—things we do not have in our humanness—to share with our offenders.

Smooth Stone #4: Drawing Near to Jesus at the Cross

Having brokenness of heart and confessing our needs of His provisions are precious to God. The actual transaction of healing grace for heart wounds takes place as we walk by faith to meet the Lord Jesus at the cross. As we lay off our wounds (and resultant feelings) that have been placed in us through unfair criticism, Jesus takes them into His bosom and bears them away from us. In the unfair exchange He takes our heartaches away and gives us the gift of healing grace, His resurrection life and power. As we embrace His gracious gifts, wounds done through unfair words are healed and cleansed, and we're given the ability to forgive the offense and the offender!

Smooth Stone #5: The Fresh Filling of the Spirit

The final stone to throw at the inner giant of unfair criticism is to invite the Spirit of Jesus to come into us in fullness and power. The Father God delights to fill us with His Spirit when we ask Him. We invite Him to stand in us, moving us to know His power to love those who have treated us badly. He gives us the power to bless those who curse us and pray for those who speak falsely against us.

As present-day overcomers of the inner giants of the heart, the best thing we can do for ourselves and our offenders is to take our wounds to the cross and experience their crucifixion with Christ. The best thing we can do for our own spiritual health is to receive the forgiveness of Jesus for the offenses and confess that forgiveness to our offenders. The power of the critical words is destroyed at the cross, and the Lord, risen with healing in His wings, lives in our heart in fullness and in power. Where He dwells in power, giants of the heart vacate the premises!

Chapter Sixteen

ℒ

Defeating the Giant of Shame

A S WE MARCH INTO the valleys—life's battlegrounds of the heart—and attack the giants we find there, we need to remember to choose the attitudes of an overcomer in Christ. Internal giants we encounter are often rooted in wounds and deeply felt hurts of the past. These internal giants war against our faith in the Lord. They hate it when we trust in and surrender to Him from the heart. They stand in direct opposition to our being people who are increasingly passionate about the kingdom of God. They rob us of joy and the desire to please God. Often when we want to walk with God and please Him, these internal giants send us the message that we aren't fit to lovingly serve God. What lies and paralysis they bring to the children of God!

It takes great courage to attack these giant-sized problems, because they have been there for a long time and we have tried unsuccessfully on numerous occasions to defeat them with human grit and determination. The difference here, which is the focus of this study, is that we aren't attacking the giants with our strength, will, grit and determination this time. Instead, we are choosing to take the biblical attitudes of faith-inspired courage and optimism, believing that God Almighty is consistently faithful to do what He has promised in His Word. We confess the facts, as David and Caleb of old did, that God is the Mighty Warrior and the battle is His. The internal victory we walk in by faith, is His gift to us through His work for us on Calvary. No giant of the human heart can remain standing when the Lord Jesus defeats it!

Armed with such courage and confidence, born in us by living faith in the Word of God, let's attack and defeat another giant that seeks to paralyze God's special sons and daughters: the internal giant of *shame*. Shame is feeling devalued in the eyes of others, feeling humiliation and embarrassment. It is an internal debt of the heart created by unkind and cruel words of blame we received from significantly respected people in our lives. The difficult thing about feeling shamed is that often we are being wounded by words for something we don't feel warranted such a response. The person inflicting the wound likely is reacting out of his or her own wounds, rather than to the specific issue at hand. The words, however, are openly humiliating, belittling us in front of others, making us feel like we were less-than, small, and not valued. When we've been repeatedly shamed by parents or people we respect, the internal message is that we are somehow a disgrace. Notice that this is very personal to us, not limited to behaviors we did or didn't do. This can lead us into endless cycles of self-defeating, self-incriminating behaviors and a lifetime of feeling worthless even though we may be quite talented, intelligent, and gifted.

Let's also be very clear about the fact that shame creates deep wounding in the heart of the victim and can have permanent effects. As a man who watches people closely, I have seen more than my share of public humiliation happen. I've watched controlling parents utterly humiliate a child in a mall in order to bring the child's behavior under control. As terribly hurtful words rain down on a child—words like, "You are such a little brat! You always embarrass me in public!" the child's behaviors may be externally controlled, but inside there's a heart that stores up those words.

> **Shame is feeling devalued in the eyes of others, feeling humiliation and embarrassment.**

I've also had the privilege of helping a lot of wonderful people to get free from this internal giant of the heart caused by punishment in front of family members. Open humiliation before the rest of one's family may get desired results of curbing a certain set of behaviors, but really deep scars are placed in the heart of a child who has experienced this repeatedly. Another illustration of shaming behaviors happened one evening at a church social. In front of a whole room full of people, a woman joked about her husband's lack of ability to please her. He laughed with everyone else, but after the laughter subsided, I watched his neck get red, and his face was downcast for the rest of the evening. The shaming wound had struck his heart. The giant was bellowing at him, mocking him and belittling him from within!

Let's consider what the Scriptures have to say about this internal giant of shame. In many ways it is like the giant of unfair criticism or slander, because it is something put in us by words that wound. Yet there are subtle differences I'd like us to consider. Shame has created a wounding that has resulted from having been publicly humiliated. Unfair criticism and slander often take place when we aren't present. Personally, I have a real problem with the veracity of that little motto "Sticks and stones can break my bones but words will never hurt me". Honestly, whoever originally came up with that and wrote it just couldn't possibly have experienced being shamed. Words can wound and can have powerful and debilitating long-term effects!

The Giant of Shame in the Bible

One of our giant-slaying heroes we have been studying is the shepherd boy who became a king, David. He was certainly no stranger to feeling shamed and publicly humiliated by people whom he loved. He wrote about this topic very candidly in Psalm 109. He poured out the original wounds and how he felt about those wounds in the text:

> O God, whom I praise, do not remain silent, for wicked and deceitful men have opened their mouths against me; they have spoken against me with lying tongues. With words of hatred they surround me; they attack me without a cause. In return for my friendship they accuse me, but I am a man of prayer. They repay me evil for good, and hatred for my friendship. (vs. 1–5)

> But you, O Sovereign Lord, deal well with me for your name's sake; out of the goodness of your love deliver me. For I am poor and needy, and my heart is wounded

within me. I fade away like an evening shadow; I am shaken off like a locust. My knees give way from fasting; my body is thin and gaunt. I am the object of scorn to my accusers; when they see me, they shake their heads. Help me, O Lord my God; save me in accordance with your love. Let them know that it is your hand, that you, O Lord, have done it. (vs. 21–27)

Can you hear the powerfully debilitating effects that shame and humiliation are having on David? He is feeling physical, emotional, mental, and spiritual lack within him as he pours out his heart to God. Look at some of his words with me:

1. He feels inner poverty, neediness, and heartsickness: "I am poor and needy, and my heart is wounded within me." His heart is overwhelmed with pain. He is struggling with how it feels to have a person you love and respect as a friend publicly humiliate him and attack him.

2. Due to having been publicly shamed, David feels lack of self-worth and feels devalued before the Lord and the people of God: "I fade like an evening shadow." His wounding makes him feel that he doesn't have substance within, doesn't matter, and is not esteemed.

3. Physically he feels tremendously weakened by an involuntary fast; food just doesn't appeal to him—it doesn't smell good or taste good. He feels achy all over because of the emotional load he's under: "I am shaken off like a locust. My knees give way from fasting; my body is thin and gaunt."

4. He feels like he is the target of massive amounts of open, public criticism and he has feelings of humiliation inside. He feels like the target of scorn and ridicule from people whom he loves: "I am an object of scorn to my accusers, when they see me they shake their heads."

That, my dear friends, is a pretty graphic picture that describes very well what shame and humiliation can do to our inner being and to our physical bodies. King David, our former teenage giant-slayer, clearly understood the internal giant of shame, didn't he? I am so thankful he put such honest and open words in his songs of praise to God in the midst of his pain. It is a precious thing to be able to look at Scripture and know we aren't alone.

> **More than one person has decided to cut and run when the feelings of shame and disgrace were too heavy to bear.**

Shame has been experienced by God's men and women down through the ages. They found the Lord's healing mercy and grace to walk in it and we can too.

It is a real life lesson that David gives us when he gets it out in a love song to God. The lesson is, don't clam up when feeling emotionally and spiritually wounded inside. Don't internalize the heartache and pretend it will go away. David took it to the throne of God and cried out to Him in prayer concerning what he was feeling in his heart. That's a great place to start remedial action, isn't it?

Wounds of shame and feeling disgraced by someone we love and respect takes an enormous toll on the heart of the victim. The embarrassment of it can make you just wish you could run away from it and start anew with a whole new group of people. More than one person has decided to cut and run when the feelings of shame and disgrace were too heavy to bear. Yet, if we truly love the person who has wounded us, escape isn't as good an option as seeking to be healed by God and reconciled to the one who did the wounding.

Shame Doesn't Get Removed by Repentance

As with other internal giants that are placed in our hearts, by words that cut and wound, the giant of shame will not be removed nor will it be destroyed by our feelings of sorrow and repentance. No amount of weeping will dissipate feelings of shame and humiliation. When wounding is done to us by others, there is nothing in us from which we are responsible to repent. It isn't a matter of our sin. It is a matter of our having been sinned against. We don't need ownership, confession, and repentance. We need to experience the healing of God's grace at the cross of Jesus. We need to experience the willful choice of laying off our wounding on Jesus at the cross and finding His precious flow of forgiveness to us that we may express it to our offender. *It is a matter of His mercy triumphing over the judgment we have felt from the one who has shamed us.* His mercy flows to us from His mercy seat.

King David understood he need to be saved and delivered by God through healing of his heart. He didn't need more remorse and sorrow, nor repentance. Listen very carefully to what he pours out to God in his prayer in this Psalm:

> But you, O Sovereign Lord, deal with me for your name's sake; out of the goodness of your love, deliver me. (vs. 21)

> Help me, O Lord my God; save me in accordance with your love. Let them know that it is your hand, that you, O Lord, have done it. (vss. 26–27)

> With my mouth I will greatly extol the Lord; in the great throng I will praise him. For he stands at the right hand of the needy one, to save his life from those who condemn him. (vss. 30–31)

David cried out to receive mercy, salvation, and deliverance as God's gift to his wounded heart. He based his petition on the facts he understood about God's faithfulness as His redeemer and strong deliverer. I am touched by the way the Lord Jehovah came to His special son and servant David and mended his wounded heart. No wonder he could write in a beautiful song of love, "Because the Lord is my Shepherd I lack nothing" (Ps. 23:1). Today, because of the revelation of Jesus Christ's redeeming work for us on the cross, we have a biblical record of His gift to us of peace with God. Jesus Christ has delivered us. The record of His work is available for us all to read, and understand, in the New Testament.

We are told He is the Lamb of God who takes away the sins of the world. That includes the ones done to us! Armed with the attitude of an overcomer by faith in Christ Jesus our Lord, let's grab our sling of faith and enter the valley of the heart where this giant of shame bellows at us, "You can't beat me!" Walk over to the brook with me and let's pick up some smooth stones for use as projectiles of the faith we can launch for maximum impact on the giant.

Smooth Stone #1: The Word of God

In the Scriptures we find many references about how precious and special we are to God. That is an aspect of the Word we need as we face the inner giant of shame and public humiliation. We need to know the truth about the Lord as it is revealed to us in Scripture. He is in fact faithful to us and loves us tremendously.

> "For I know the plans I have for you," declares the Lord, "plans to prosper you and not to harm you, plans to give you hope and a future. Then you will call upon me and come and pray to me, and I will listen to you. You will seek me and find me when you seek me with all your heart. I will be found by you' declares the Lord." (Jer. 29:11–14a)

In the tremendous security of the love of God, we also need to know how He feels about His own sons and daughters in Christ. We need His opinion of us as a sense of positive self-perception, especially when we have been repeatedly wounded with shame and humiliation. Paul wrote to the Roman believers, regarding their having put their trust in the Lord Jesus for their salvation: "Anyone who trusts in him will never be put to shame." God doesn't shame and condemn His children, as human parents sometimes do. When He disciplines or corrects, it is always done with a hope of life change. Paul also wrote to the Galatian believers about the tremendous biblical truth of our spiritual adoption into His family:

> But when the time had fully come, God sent his Son, born of a woman, born under law, to redeem those under law, that we might receive the full rights of sons. Because you are sons, God sent the Spirit of His Son into our hearts, the Spirit who calls out "Abba, Father." So you are no longer a slave but a son; and since you are a son, God has made you also an heir. (Gal. 4:4–7)

> **God doesn't shame and condemn His children, as human parents sometimes do. When He disciplines or corrects, it is always done with a hope of life change.**

You can count on it, brothers and sisters, that what He has said to you and about you in Scripture is truth, and He stands behind it! He is faithful to you. He loves you with an everlasting love and draws you with chords of kindness. He will even take the hurts and the heartaches of life as crucibles of love that have a tutorial impact on you. As He releases you from inner prisons of the heart, He works to help you to achieve your fullest potential for His kingdom.

Smooth Stone #2: Brokenness of Heart

Knowing how He feels about you will really help you to see how damaging the human offenses of shaming have been. Allow the brokenness you feel inside to draw you to see, in the light of His awesome provisions for you, your human frailty and weakness to provide healing for yourself. Remember, the truth of the matter is that He longs for us to know the joy of being transformed into the image of Christ Jesus. As long as we focus on what we can do for ourselves, He is not free to raise up the life of Jesus in us. He is free to raise up the life of Jesus Christ in us by His Spirit only when we have chosen to be broken in heart regarding our ways. If there are ways we are hiding sins committed against us, we should want to know why we do this. Why do we want to hold on to the offense? Why not face the need of forgiveness for the offender? God is much more concerned that we walk in His ways than that we are comfortable in life. Allow brokenness to deliver its message and, by faith, find His smile of grace.

Smooth Stone #3: Confession of Our Need

Again it doesn't take the intelligence of a rocket scientist to figure out that we really do need to talk it out with God when we feel shame and humiliation. If you have trouble praying it out, telling God how you feel regarding your offender, get someone who knows and loves you to help you pray through it. These feelings will hold us prisoner if we permit them. They must be confessed in order for the feelings of anger and frustration to be taken out of our hearts.

Smooth Stone #4: Drawing Near to Jesus at the Cross

There at the cross of Jesus our Lord, we choose to come to Him and lay off on Him the wounds of shame and unforgiveness. He takes into Himself all that is in us that is offensive to the Father God. Our actions taken there by faith in Jesus literally destroy our mortal enemy Satan's power in the wounds of shame and humiliation. He and his tempting spirits lose their ability to imprison us with the things done to us in the past. That includes the issue of having experienced the shame and humiliation of loved ones. As God's sons and daughters we can walk to the cross by faith and lay in the bosom of Jesus what has held us prisoner of the inner giants of the heart. Then Jesus bears them away from us, forever. Through the unfair exchange that God the Spirit does for us there, we are healed and cleansed; we are given the ability to forgive both the offense and the offender!

Without a doubt, our Lord Jesus Christ took upon Himself our shame on the cross. The author of the Book of Hebrews is careful to point this out to us in chapter 12:2:

> Let us fix our eyes on Jesus, the author and perfecter of our faith, who for the joy set before him *endured the cross, scorning its shame,* and sat down at the right hand of the throne of God. (emphasis mine)

Smooth Stone #5: The Fresh Filling of the Spirit

The final stone to throw by faith at the internal giant shame, is the decision to invite the Holy Spirit to come and dwell in fullness and in power in my life. We literally invite Him to stand in us in the very valley of the heart where shame and disgrace once stood. He brings the opinion of the Father and the Son to us as inner Counselor of the heart. We are called to walk in concert with Him: "Since we live by the Spirit let us keep in step with the Spirit." He makes it possible for us to bless those who have cursed us with wounds of shame and humiliation. What a joy to walk in His ways and provisions, the Word of God being a living reality in our hearts.

Let me say something to you, giant-slayer, that I have said before. The greatest thing you can do for yourself is to decide to allow God the Spirit to make His ways and provisions a deep reality in your life. Jesus Christ is the only burden bearer in the kingdom of God. You aren't designed by God to carry burdens around on your shoulders, nor to live with the wounds significant people have placed in you. Please, for your own good as well as your offender's, permit brokenness, confession, the unfair exchange, and the fresh filling God's Spirit to raise you to new levels of victory over the inner giants of the heart.

You are really becoming quite proficient at stone throwing, aren't you?

Chapter Seventeen

❧

Defeating the Giant
of Rejection

A S WE FACE OUR FOURTH giant of the heart imposed on us by others, I want to remind you of several factors that are really important to the process of attacking and defeating inner giants. Our models for overcoming giants in our lives have been the six Old Testament giant-slayers we studied in chapter two. Those men clearly understood some faith issues we'd better have in perspective as well. When we have a personal relationship with the Lord by faith, we walk according to the principles of His kingdom found in His Word. We understand that the attitudes with which we face life are something we choose to embrace regardless of our circumstances. We cannot choose our circumstances in life, but we can and must choose the attitude with which we will face them.

Faith will give birth to courage and optimism in our hearts and lives when it lives in us, just as faith birthed courage in the Old Testament giant-slayers. According to the Word of God, He delights in people who will trust Him for all of their needs in life, including the tough ones. He strongly supports His children by His Spirit when we are wholly committed to Him.

In this chapter, we are looking at the inner giant of the heart imposed upon us by others: *rejection*. Rejection is a powerful giant, often dwelling in wounds that began with words or actions that are outside our control. Then the wounds find their way into our hearts and dwell there. To have experienced rejection from a significant person in our lives is to have been refused the gift of acceptance and being valued. It is to have been refused, or turned away from, by someone we've loved deeply or respected highly. Rejection communicates to us that we are cast aside as somehow being unacceptable, faulty, defective. When rejection comes to us, it wounds us because we so deeply love the person from whom we receive it. Precisely because we love so much, rejection cuts and scars us for life unless we experience the healing grace we can only find in Christ Jesus.

In our culture there are a plethora of people who are living with the inner debts of the heart that are caused by having been rejected by people they loved—people whose opinions were cherished and who were trusted deeply. Approval from these esteemed individuals was vital to the sense of well-being of the rejectee. These wounds run very deep and can have permanent effects on the wounded person's life.

Rejection has run amok in our culture today—from adult children of divorce . . . to adults who had been adopted in childhood . . . to people who had a parent they couldn't please . . . to those whose dads rarely affirmed them and based their value on how well they performed . . . to the child whose mother felt that her reputation as a homemaker was more important than giving hugs and kisses . . . to spouses who are blindsided by a mate's affair and demand divorce . . . to the man or woman who lives with a mate who constantly criticizes them and whose expectations cannot be met. Rejection's deep emotional debt load, carried in the human heart, is of vital concern to people who help people today.

People Who Suffer from Having Been Rejected

Without question, the place where most inner wounds occur is in the context of family. Rejection in the family produces tremendous wounding of the heart, mind, and soul of the spouse or the child. The reason this is so is that we receive the set of lenses through which we view all of life from our family. We learn to deal with issues of life either by faith or from a perspective of having been wounded.

In a healthy, strong family the members learn to deal with each other within the parameters of the fact of being loved. The healthy family sends the message in a thousand different ways: "Regardless of conflict or painful circumstances you are loved, and even while this issue is being worked through, you still will be valued as part of us and we will be here for you." The members learn they are loved and cherished regardless of how they feel while walking through a particular issue or season of conflict. Healthy families attack and solve problems. They view each other as a part of the whole family and family members with whom they presently may be in conflict are seen as teammates.

In unhealthy family settings, the individual family members experience rejection from others in their family unit. The message these families give each other and receive from each other is, "I'm refusing to accept you anymore." When people who should be there for us reject us, the debts established in the heart, mind, and soul of that person are deep-seated and debilitating feelings of insecurity. The person may spend an entire lifetime living with, or trying to live down, the malignant thought the enemy implanted through family rejection: *If I get too close here I'm only going to end up getting hurt again.* Distrust and suspicion of people, when nurtured in the heart, tend to view others as potential sources of pain instead of potential life partners and friends.

Rejection from key people in our lives—people we love and respect highly—leads to damaged emotions. Public words that wound, even in the family setting, can place debts in the human heart that cause the recipient to hear and feel the debilitating message of the enemy: "There is something terribly wrong with me." It can lead to an inability to enter into deep, meaningful relationships of love and trust because we perceive them as potentially permanent.

Lack of self-worth from wounds of rejection can lead a person on an endless treadmill of human performance for acceptance in the family, the workplace, and the church. Rejection can freeze our emotions with fear of being hurt again. Sometimes people enter into relationships with an inner tendency to view others as potential adversaries to be watched closely, as opposed to potential friends or people with whom they may enter meaningful relationships, finding intimacy and a sense of belonging and acceptance. Rejection can produce a hurt-before-you-get-hurt mentality, flowing from a lifetime of distrust and suspicion.

These debts of distrust and suspicion can make it nigh unto impossible to enter into a deeply satisfying walk with the Lord Jesus, causing us to perpetually doubt the faithfulness and the grace of God. These emotions, when present in us, only pay lip service to grace. They can't grasp the meaning of grace, of being accepted into God's family as an adopted son or daughter, dearly loved by God. Damaged emotions are often frozen by fear and the inability to relate meaningfully to the Lord, myself, or others. These frozen, damaged emotions keep us from entering into permanent, trusting relationships. Damaged emotions need the healing touch of the mercy and grace of God in Christ Jesus our Lord.

> **Distrust and suspicion of people, when nurtured in the heart, tend to view others as potential sources of pain instead of potential life partners and friends.**

Rejection and the Heart of God

The issue I want you to think through with me is that God understands very well what it feels like to be rejected by those whom we love with searching, reaching, intense love. His overtures of mercy and grace to people, His kindness and love for us, have been rejected for thousands of years by those who should surely know better.

The Lord gave the children of Israel His physical presence with them as He led them out of Egypt. He was a pillar of fire by night and cloud by day. He gave them tremendous miracles of divine intervention to bring them into the land He had promised their forefathers. He gave them the Canaan Land as a place in which He would live with them, as a Father with His children. They would be His special people, chosen by Him to serve Him and to reveal His holiness and love to the neighboring countries.

In the story of God's people and their view of being ruled personally by God, there is an interesting turn of events in 1 Samuel 8. There the people of God came to Samuel, God's prophet, and rejected being *merely Jehovah's people!* Their complaint was that they wanted to be like every other nation. They wanted to be free to name their own king and do their own thing. They rejected serving God only. They wanted their own human systems to follow. In the process they broke the Father's heart, because He understood, far better than they, the ramifications of their decision. Can you feel His heartache?

> And the Lord told Samuel, "Listen to all the people are saying to you; it is not you they have rejected, but they have rejected me as their king. As they have done from the day I brought them up out of Egypt until this day, forsaking me and serving other gods, so they are doing to you." (vs. 7–8)

The majestic and merciful Lord God Almighty carried them in His arms, and sought to show them the truth of their blessings and rewards for walking in His ways. This majestic God who promised them a fruitful life and victory over any enemy that opposed them, this gracious Father, experienced their rejection. Instead of knowing Him personally, they wanted a human ruler.

Lest we think the rejection of God ended in the Old Testament, lets consider the life of our Jesus. His mission was one of mercy and grace. He came to us to assume our sins and guilt. He came to take unto Himself our humanity and go to a cross and die for us as our sacrificial Lamb. One would certainly think we would treat the Son of God with love and acceptance. Let's look at the record of human treatment of Him. There is reference after reference to the fact that we inflicted on Him the pain of rejecting the One who came to die for us:

> He was despised and rejected by men, a man of sorrows, and familiar with suffering. Like one from whom men hide their faces he was despised, and we esteemed him not. (Isa. 53:3)

> Jesus left there and went to his hometown, accompanied by his disciples. When the Sabbath came, he began to teach in the synagogue, and many who heard him were amazed. "Where did this man get these things?" they asked. "What's this wisdom that has been given him, that he even does miracles! Isn't this the carpenter? Isn't this Mary's son and the brother of James, Joseph, Judas and Simon? Aren't his sisters here with us?" And they took offense at him. Jesus said to them, "Only in his hometown, among his relatives and in his own house is a prophet without honor." He could not do any miracles there, except lay his hand on a few sick people and heal them. And he was amazed at their lack of faith. (Mark 6:1–5)

The point of these scriptures is to have us see and understand that Jesus, on His mission of mercy to bear our sins and die for us on the cross, was rejected by the very people for whom He came to die. In fact, the history of God's people on this planet is that we, who have known better, have rejected His love again and again. We have taken our own way and devised our human systems to serve Him. God's children—Old Testament Israel and the New Testament church—have left behind us an incredible legacy of rejecting and forsaking God time and again. Yet God continues to reach out to us in mercy and grace. In fact, because of His tremendous love for us, God the Father even used the hurt of our rejection as a means of making His Son Jesus a merciful High Priest, who is able to sympathize with us:

> But we see Jesus, now crowned with glory and honor because he suffered death, so that by the grace of God he might taste death for everyone. In bringing many sons to God it was fitting that God . . . should make the author of their salvation perfect through suffering. (Heb. 2:9–10)

> For we do not have a high priest who is unable to sympathize with our weaknesses, but we have one who has been tempted in every way—just as we are—yet was without sin. Let us then approach the throne of grace with confidence, so that we may receive mercy and find grace to help us in our time of need. (Heb. 4:15–16)

We have a Master, our Lord Jesus, who has experienced the terrible pain of the heart and mind caused by rejection from those He loved. In fact, He was rejected by those for whom He died. You and I can talk things out with Him and know He understands. We can tell Him exactly how we feel when we've been rejected. He will listen to us and feel our heart's needs with compassion, sympathy, and empathy. He is a great High Priest who is touched with even the feelings of our infirmities. We will always find acceptance in His heart at the throne of grace. That is a truth of the Word of God upon which all of us can depend. God reveals Himself in Scripture as loving, kind, full of mercy and grace. We are accepted in His family as adopted sons and daughters, just as we are. He will begin with us at the point of our need and transform us into the image of His Son Jesus by the power of His Holy Spirit.

> ... because of His tremendous love for us, God the Father even used the hurt of our rejection as a means of making His Son Jesus a merciful High Priest, who is able to sympathize with us.

When it comes to deciding to face and defeat this tremendously powerful internal giant of the heart that has been imposed upon us by people we love, it is important that we begin with a foundation of acceptance. Rejection is another inner giant for which confession and repentance do not help. It is not a sin issue for which we have guilt. The nagging debts of the heart that are placed in us by others give us the internal message, "There's something wrong with me." These are rooted in our emotions because rejection creates wounds. Wounds can't be fixed through repentance. They must be healed. The cross of Jesus Christ our Lord is the place of healing to which we must go. The giant of rejection is destroyed by healing grace and by the acceptance of the Father, in and through the finished work of Jesus on the cross. Grab your sling of faith, walk over to the brook with me, and let's gather some smooth stones.

Smooth Stone #1: The Word of God

When the giant of rejection lives in our hearts we have experienced deep wounding because we have loved deeply. The thing we really need to fight against this inner giant, is a deep foundation stone of having received unconditional love and acceptance. The need we have for acceptance must first be found by us in the One who matters the most, our Father God. All of God's sons and daughters must come to experience the joy and liberty of playing to an audience of one (God) in whom we find grace, mercy, and love. From the bedrock of His acceptance, we are set free to embrace transformation into what He has designed for us when He created us. The holy and awesome God accepts me, loves me, and has adopted me as His child. Please listen to the Counselor, who lives in your heart, as He works in you to give you anointed understanding of these Scriptures, and hundreds like them:

> Be imitators of God, therefore, *as dearly loved children* and live a life of love, just as Christ loved us and gave himself up for us as a fragrant offering and sacrifice to God. (Eph 5:1–2, emphasis mine)

> But now, this is what the Lord says—he who created you, O Jacob, he who formed you, O Israel: "Fear not, for I have redeemed you; I have summoned you by name;

you are mine. When you pass through the waters, I will be with you; and when you pass through the rivers, they will not sweep over you. When you walk through the fire, you will not be burned; the flames will not set you ablaze. For I am the Lord, your God, the Holy One of Israel, your Savior; . . . *Since you are precious and honored in my sight and because I love you.*" (Isa. 43:1–4a, emphasis mine)

The Lord has taken away your punishment, he has turned back your enemy. The Lord, the King of Israel is with you; *never again will you fear any harm.* On that day they will say to Jerusalem, 'Do not fear, O Zion; do not let your hands hang limp. *The Lord your God is with you,* he is mighty to save. *He will take great delight in you, he will quiet you with his love, he will rejoice over you with singing.*' (Zeph. 3:15–17, emphasis mine)

Accept one another, then, *just as Christ accepted you,* in order to bring praise to God. (Rom. 15:7, emphasis mine)

Smooth Stone #2: Brokenness of Heart

I want to remind you that having a broken and contrite heart is a special thing to God. The wounding and heartache created by rejection can be used as a tool to draw us nearer to God the Father's tremendous love and mercy. Brokenness of heart can be a messenger of grace if we permit it. Remember this scriptural fact: God loves you and longs for fellowship with you. When you and I get beyond our means of providing for ourselves, when wounds break us within and we surrender deeply to Him in brokenness, He is moved with compassion and mercy and ministers to us by His Spirit.

Smooth Stone #3: Confession of Our Need

Wounds from rejection by others can exist in places where the enemy has placed debilitating lies into our hearts. What we are feeling is an inner reality of the heart. These untrue emotions and thoughts we believe about ourselves can live only in the darkness of our hearts if we permit them. They must be owned, brokenness of heart embraced, and confession of our needs made to God. The prince of darkness and all of his beings lose their power when we bring out into the light, by confession to God, what they held in darkness in our hearts.

Smooth Stone #4: Drawing Near to Jesus at the Cross

This is the place where the wounds of rejection actually are destroyed. This transaction between you and the Lord Jesus may take quite a while to complete. But the joy of walking in freedom from the wounds and in the acceptance of the Father is worth the work you'll do there with Jesus. When we walk by faith to the cross of Jesus and place, through confession, into His bosom the rejection we've experienced from others, along with the emotions we feel and the lies we believe about ourselves, Jesus takes them and destroys them. Scripture is clear that all sins are

> Scripture is clear that all sins are destroyed in Jesus Christ the Lord at the cross.

destroyed in Jesus Christ the Lord at the cross. That includes the sins of rejection committed by those whom we have loved and respected. I plead with you to go to the cross of Jesus and, by faith, lay the wounds and the offenders in His bosom there. Watch Him take the wounds and the offenses out of you and into Himself, crucifying them, destroying them.

Smooth Stone #5: Being Filled Anew with the Holy Spirit

The Father God delights to give the Holy Spirit to those who desire Him. Invite Him to come into your heart anew, there at the cross of Jesus. Ask the Holy Spirit to wash you with fresh cleansing in your heart from all the offenses that were put there. He empowers you to live above all of the wounds and heartaches of your yesterdays. Hear Him grant you forgiveness there for those who have hurt you so deeply. Take into your heart His life, His righteousness, His mercy and forgiveness. Embrace, through Him, the power to love and enjoy meaningful relationships with people, the ability to risk loving and trusting again.

The inner giant of rejection, the wounds of the past, and the crippling effects of damaged emotions do not have to live in us. You and I don't have to put up with this inner giant of the heart who stands there shouting defiantly at us, "You can't beat me!" Take your weapons of truth and your attitudes of faith, courage, and optimism, and march out into the valleys of the heart and cut down rejection!

Having cut down the giant of rejection in your own heart, go one step further and give the precious gift of acceptance to others. Take the risk to trust and love others. We experience deeper grace from Him when we give away to others what He has given to us. Jesus told His followers, "Freely you have received, freely give" (Matt. 10:8). You can do it. I know you can.

Chapter Eighteen

⟢

Defeating the Giant
of Legalism

THROUGHOUT THIS STUDY we have been focusing on the fact that attitude is a choice we all make. The Lord has given us the gift of living by faith because we have become His sons and daughters. He began His work in us by bringing us the truth about ourselves, about Him, and about our need of grace because of sins. He carries on His work in our hearts and perfects us the same way. He ministers to us with His Word anointed to our hearts, and He gives us the opportunity to cooperate with His will through faith. Attitudes born in us because we believe Him—to do beyond what we can ask or imagine—include courage and optimism regardless of the obstacles before us.

Our model has been the Old Testament giant-slayers, such as David and Caleb, who attacked formidable obstacles in the name of the Lord. They are such powerful examples for us, demonstrating that faith will inspire attitudes of courage and optimism. These men chose to believe God and His ability to give them victory over their foes, while others around them cowered in fear and huddled in defensive postures. We have studied their choices to walk with God and have noted several things worth looking at one more time:

1. According to military strategies and human reasoning, these men faced what people around them had verified as insurmountable. According to mere human understanding, these men were out of their minds!
2. They chose to live by faith. They saw their battles ahead of them as spiritual confrontations brought against them by the enemy. Their trust was in the Lord God and in His ability to deliver them, not in their resources or lack thereof.
3. They chose not to believe the giant's testimony about themselves. When a giant bellowed, "You can't beat me!" they didn't accept it as fact.
4. They were mightily used of God in the midst of incredibly difficult battles of life.

Like those giants-slayers of the Old Testament, we often face things in life that are very difficult. Life can be unfair to God's people at times. Choosing to face giants of adversity and difficulty in our lives begins with being overcomers in our hearts. Remember the basic premise of this book: there must be smaller victories within before we'll see victories in bigger issues of life that we all must face.

In this section of the book, we are facing giants of the heart that are imposed on us by people we love. In this chapter, we are looking at our final giant: *legalism.* This giant of the heart is placed there by our acceptance of the contents of the teachings of human beings. There is a fine line between tradition, which is wonderful and alive, and traditionalism, which is backward focused and based in human thinking. Tradition is the living faith of those who have gone before us, while traditionalism is the dead faith of those who are living off of yesterday's blessings.

Legalism is to follow a set of rules, laws, or standards, believing that by following these rules one gains special standing with God. Legalism is often taught as the Word of God, but the rules taught by people are based on interpretations of Scripture that are often poor at best. Legalism's promise is attainment of correct standing before God, but it doesn't deliver the goods. Essentially what legalism does is use guilt motivation to get its adherents to perform certain behaviors. The thing it really establishes in the hearts of its adherents, is a system of internal debts. It creates a tyranny of the I-ought-to-do syndrome, of living for the fickle blessing of what others may think or say. It is totally concerned with the outward expression and the appearance of one's Christian life before people. Its significant watchword is *obedience*

> **Legalism is to follow a set of rules, laws, or standards, believing that by following these rules one gains special standing with God.**

that focuses on human grit and determination This is in contrast and direct opposition to the love-inspired obedience that flows from a heart that adores and reveres God.

From my observation, what generally happens is that there's a slow growth of legalism over several generations. A movement begins with a definitive work and outpouring of the Holy Spirit in the hearts of members of a group. They experience profound brokenness and accompanying life change as He works in their hearts. A number of these life-changing things are new "ways" of the Lord and these are embraced in the lifestyle of the people because they have deeply surrendered to Him. When these are passed on to the next generation, they are fresh from the working of God's Spirit in the speakers' hearts and lives. The next generation gets the "way" of the Lord without having had the powerful life-changing experience with the Lord. By the time this "way" gets passed to the third generation, it is merely a set of rules or standards taught by people as a legalistic approach to life. Different groups have different things on their elaborate lists of "things not to do" or "places not to go," as well as the to-do lists. These things often are defended by turning to the Scriptures with some rather interesting interpretive techniques.

The Religious Leaders of Jesus' Day Specialized in Legalism

The Scribes and Pharisees of Jesus' day had made a science of legalistic thinking, seeking to attain righteousness by observing an elaborate system of rules and regulations. There are many scripture passages in the Gospels to which we could turn in order to study this issue in their lives, and therefore, learn the foundational issues upon which legalism stands.

I want to just highlight two such passages from Matthew's Gospel. In chapter 15, verses 1–20, there is a dialogue between Jesus and the religious leaders. They are demanding to know why He doesn't observe the traditions of the elders. Jesus replies,

> And why do you break the command of God for the sake of your tradition? For God said, "Honor your father and mother" and "Anyone who curses his father or mother must be put to death." But you say that if a man says to his father or mother "Whatever help you might otherwise have received from me is a gift devoted to God," he is not to honor his father with it. Thus you nullify the word of God for the sake of your tradition. You hypocrites! (vss. 3–7)

I don't think one has to read too much into this passage to see and understand the fact that Jesus was very confrontational with their presupposition that they could attain righteousness by their own efforts. He called them hypocrites who literally stood against God's Word (which they claimed to uphold) by way of their tradition. In regard to righteousness being an issue of the heart, Jesus concluded later with His disciples,

> Don't you see that whatever enters the mouth goes into the stomach and then out of the body? But the things that come out of the mouth come from the heart, and these make a man "unclean." For out of the heart come evil thoughts, murder, adultery, sexual immorality, theft, false testimony, slander. These are what make a man

"unclean"; but eating with unwashed hands does not make him "unclean." (vss. 17–20)

A second passage that is included in the Gospel of Matthew that really gets at this issue of legalism is found in Matthew 23. In that passage the Lord Jesus entered into scathing rebuke of the religious status quo of the day. There are "woes" pronounced on these religious icons who were concerned merely with how they appeared to others. Seven times the Lord Jesus denounced them with the words "Woe to you teachers of the law and Pharisees, you hypocrites!" For the Lord Jesus, doing things to be viewed as righteous by others is totally useless and thoroughly disdained by God. His desire is first for truth in the inward parts where only God and the individual can see. After the heart has been cleansed and changed by the love of God, behaviors will automatically change.

One of the lead Pharisees of the day was a man named Saul of Tarsus (a city in Cilicia). Saul was on the road of pursuing legalistic righteousness by keeping all of the manmade traditions of the elders. He was progressing in his religious zeal and advancing toward becoming a leading Pharisee. He understood righteousness to be a function of keeping rules that had been passed to him by human beings. This understanding had left him full of hatred for anybody who didn't keep the traditions of the elders—traditions he perceived to be synonymous with the Law of God. He even went so far as to persecute, imprison, and kill Christians, whom he considered to be a threat to his religious way of life. He was beating, imprisoning and in some cases voting to kill believers, all under the false assumption that he was pleasing God. Listen to his testimony of the folly of legalistic righteousness after he truly met the Lord Jesus:

> If anyone else thinks he has reasons to put confidence in the flesh, I have more: circumcised on the eighth day, of the people of Israel, of the tribe of Benjamin, a Hebrew of Hebrews; in regard to the law, a Pharisee; as for zeal, persecuting the church; as for legalistic righteousness, faultless. But whatever was to my profit I now consider loss for the sake of Christ. What is more, I consider everything a loss compared to the surpassing greatness of knowing Christ Jesus my Lord, for whose sake I have lost all things. I consider them rubbish, that I may gain Christ, and be found in him, not having a righteousness of my own that comes from the law, but that which is through faith in Christ—the righteousness that comes from God and is by faith. (Phil. 3:4b–9)

For the Lord Jesus, doing things to be viewed as righteous by others is totally useless and thoroughly disdained by God.

Legalism—the keeping of endless human rules and regulations taught by people—certainly didn't work for the apostle Paul (formerly Saul). He recognized he was zealous for God at the beginning. Yet later in his life, he realized that his zeal was totally misplaced, to the point of persecuting to death those who didn't agree with his theological positions. There's a fair amount of Phariseeism in the Church of Jesus today. It very often masquerades under the guise of concern for doctrinal purity. When someone's position on Christian orthodoxy causes us to hate them and brand their position as heresy, we have ugly Phariseeism in the body of Christ!

> There's a fair amount of Phariseeism in the Church of Jesus today. It very often masquerades under the guise of concern for doctrinal purity.

The Spiritual Truth about Legalism

There are several things that are foundational to the issue of just how foolish it is to think we can attain a righteous standing before God through the legalistic performance of lists of rules or laws. The first thing is that legalism places us under the influence of guilt or negative motivation of the heart. We are always operating from a defensive posture of fear. The constant and nagging question is, "What if I fail?" This inner tyranny to guilt motivation can and often does place us in a perpetual state of insecurity. This is the real issue. Legalism results in insecurity because it doesn't answer the following: if we are dependent on our own works of obedience to know we are saved or that

264

we're living the Christian life, how do we know how much is enough? How do we know we have tipped the scale of heavenly justice in our favor? What scoring system of works do we use? Who sets the rules, and how do we know we've got the rulebook God wants us to have?

The second thing about legalism that is absolutely true was written by a man who had lived with the tyranny of performance in his heart for many years until he finally met the Lord Jesus in person and was given His righteousness by faith. The apostle Paul wrote that legalism places in the hearts of its practitioners a cloud of oppression because of the "curse of performing the law":

> You foolish Galatians! Who has bewitched you? Before your very eyes Jesus Christ was portrayed as crucified. I would like to learn just one thing from you: Did you receive the Spirit by observing the law, or by believing what you heard? Are you so foolish? After beginning with the Spirit, are you now trying to attain your goal by human effort? Have you suffered so much for nothing—if it really was for nothing? Does God give you his Spirit and work miracles among you because you observe the law, or because you believe what you heard? . . . All who rely on observing the law are under a curse, for it is written: "Cursed is everyone who does not continue to do everything written in the Book of the Law." Clearly no one is justified before God by the law, because, "The righteous will live by faith." (Gal. 3: 1–5, 10–11)

The third and final thing I'll mention here is that legalism renders us servants to external performance as we attempt to meet human agendas. Legalism does nothing to address the real issues of the heart. It ultimately results in the enslavement of people to the opinions of other people. It definitely does not lead to the life of God's Spirit breathing spiritual vitality and passion into our heart. We may keep an elaborate system of laws and rules in our outer world and yet harbor sinful desires in our heart. Legalism is works based. It says to its followers, "If you know the right and do the right, you will be living in the blessings of God." God's Word says, "The one who loves me is the one who obeys me." One is motivated by duty and obligation, while the other is motivated by love. While seeming to be saying the same thing, the two motives are miles apart.

We absolutely cannot live the Christian life by our own grit, will, and determination. The one crucial truth we all must find out for ourselves is that only the Lord Jesus Himself could ever live a life that was pleasing to God. Only Jesus could say at the end of His life, "Father, I have completed the task you sent me to accomplish." It naturally follows, then, that the only way for me to live a life that is pleasing to the Father is to do so by His Spirit who lives in me. Here's a key principle that my own repetitive failures have taught me: *My job is not to make every effort to live a Christlike life. It is to come to the cross and surrender my will to His will because only Jesus can be Jesus in me!*

If we are going to attack and defeat this giant of the heart, legalism, we will need to own some biblical truth about what it really means to live the Christian life. We are going to need our sling of faith and our shepherd's bag with five smooth stones in it to throw at legalism. I think it's about time for some of God's special sons and daughters to shed some giant-sized legalistic baggage. So let's get at it!

Smooth Stone #1: The Word of God

The weapon of the Word of God has much to say about the issues of legalism—our attempting to be righteous by keeping a set of rules taught by human beings. There are two passages I want to point us to as really key for having maximum impact on the forehead of this inner giant:

> For it is by grace you have been saved, through faith— and this is not from yourselves, it is the gift of God—not by works, so that no one can boast. For we are God's workmanship, created in Christ Jesus to do good works, which God prepared in advance for us to do. (Eph. 2:8–10)

> You who are trying to be justified by law have been alienated from Christ; you have fallen away from grace. But by faith we eagerly await through the Spirit the righteousness for which we hope. For in Christ Jesus neither circumcision nor uncircumcision has any value. The only thing that counts is faith expressing itself through love. You were running a good race. Who cut in on you and kept you from obeying the truth? (Gal. 5:4–7)

Smooth Stone #2: Brokenness of the Heart

If you see legalism or areas of human attempts at being the "best Christian I can be," allow the Spirit of God to show you the real issues that are going on inside you. The Lord is after a heart that is broken and soft before Him. "The sacrifices of God are a broken spirit, a broken and contrite heart, O God, you will not despise" (Psalms 51:17). Allow brokenness to bring its true message to you. There may be areas of unsurrendered pride in human accomplishments, or the tyranny of wanting to be accepted and of working for the approval of human beings. Permit the Spirit of God to break your heart that you might see yourself and your needs before Him.

Smooth Stone #3: Confession of Our Needs

The second step, in this process of destroying this inner giant of legalism's grip on our hearts, is the confession of our needs. He desires truth in the inward parts of our lives. He delights in our choice to bring out into the light what the enemy has used in the darkness, and what we have held in silence. To confess what we see in our hearts exposes those things to the light of Jesus Christ our Lord.

Smooth Stone #4: Drawing Near to Jesus at the Cross

Brokenness and confession of our needs are important but incomplete unless we choose to come to the cross of Jesus and lay in His bosom the issues that have held us prisoners of the heart. Anything we bring to Him, by faith, and lay in Him at the cross is destroyed by His substitutionary death for us. Many of us have walked through life with inner debts and tyranny to the opinions of people, rendering us at the mercy of legalistic teachings. Both the initial wounding, the longing for acceptance, and the issues of our human striving for self-attained righteousness must be put to death for us at the cross! What is crucified with Christ, dies!

Smooth Stone #5: The Fresh Infilling of the Holy Spirit

This is the fifth and final stone that destroys the inner giant of legalism. The destruction of human endeavor is important, but we will revert to the ways with which we are comfortable unless we are full of His loving presence. To invite Him to come to us and raise up His desires in our hearts and to produce in us the fruit of righteousness, is to have truly come to the end of ourselves and our attempts to make our own way. The Holy Spirit's role in the world and in the Christian's life is to make Jesus real, to bring to our remembrance all that He has said. He Himself living His life in me by His Spirit is the true Christian life that Scripture teaches. It is definitively relational and experiential. Christ in me, the hope of glory!

Well, my fellow giant-slayer, there you have them. Five smooth stones to throw at the inner giant of legalism. This miserable giant has led to a great amount of inner heartache for the children of God. I want to encourage you with every ounce of His strength dwelling in my heart. Cut this giant down to size. With the opportunity to walk in the light of God's love and experience a deepening relationship with Him, it is unthinkable that we should waste another day in the tyranny of legalism. What human beings think about us is secondary in importance to what God thinks. We must master the art of playing primarily to an audience of One! Throw some stones for maximum impact!

By faith, as we've walked through this study together, we have faced and defeated many giants of the heart and life. These giants can be terrible taskmasters. They must be faced and destroyed if we are to live in Christ's provisions. Giants are destroyed by faith in the awesome God who has adopted us as His sons and daughters and whom we serve. Are you feeling more comfortable with your sling of faith?

Conclusion

✍

Permitting God to Raise Up the Image of Jesus in Me

IN THIS FINAL CHAPTER, I want to share with you the reason why slaying inner giants of the heart is so important. The goal of attacking and defeating giants of the heart is to put us at a place of walking in deepening surrender to the Holy Spirit. It is the role and the function of the Spirit of God to make manifest the life and ministry of Jesus. As He lives in the sons and daughters of God, He works in us to raise up in us the image of Jesus Christ our Lord. Under the leadership of the Holy Spirit, we are more than conquerors through Him who loves us. We choose to face and attack the inner giants of the heart by faith in the works Jesus accomplished for us on the cross.

The giants of the heart are barriers the enemy wants to use to keep us from a productive walk of faith with God. They are issues of human wounding or enemy-inspired attacks that will have the effect of holding us in inner prisons if they are left unchallenged. With the successful attack and defeat of each inner giant of the heart, the human wounding and the enemy-occupied territory within us is diminished. God the Holy Spirit is given more and more room in our hearts and lives to do His works. The presence of the Lord Jesus is made more evident in our hearts and lives as we walk in deepening surrender to Him.

The Bible is the story of God's incredible drawing love, mercy and grace. Scripture teaches us about the Immanuel Principle, which is God's desire to live with His children, to know us, and be known by us. Again and again He came to His people with a desire to walk with them, dwell among them, and have them know Him as their personal God. He established His people, Israel, to be a kingdom of priests, a holy nation of people who were wholly His. Through their lives, the other nations around them would see His blessing on them and would want to know Him too. The Israelites failed miserably at their primary reason for existence and became idolatrous like the nations around them.

In the New Testament, the church is the people of God, through whom He wants to demonstrate His blessing and reach those who have yet to meet Him. Within the history of the church, there have been days of great outpourings of the Spirit of God on the earth. At these times, the life of Christ was clearly evident in the people of God. In such times of powerful moves of God's Spirit, thousands have been brought into His family. Then, in contrast, there have been other times of human agendas, spiritual idolatry, materialism, and the ways of humankind, which have resulted in the marring of and failure in our mission. During these periods in the church's history, God's presence had seemingly withdrawn, and the enemy's footprints were all over the church.

The Bible also is a record of two different ways human-kind has responded to God's overtures of love and mercy. There are clearly two paths people have chosen, down through biblical history in their attempts to seek to know God's blessing on their lives.

The first group of people are those who seek to know God by doing things for Him. These are people who see the Scriptures as primarily a set of standards to be carried out by human grit, will, and determination. These persons have as their key watchwords *obedience, obligation,* and *duty.* They have a set of rules to live by that they believe have been time-tested and if perfectly adhered to, will result in a life that is blessed of God.

However, what really happens in the keeping of the rules is an inner debt system, based on guilt motivation. The concept that only God can change the affections of the heart, causing it to desire holiness, is never addressed. The basis of their living is what they can do for God, and that is not a healthy basis for life. It is doomed to failure from the start. No person, by human grit or determination, can serve God acceptably. Only Jesus Christ our Lord was able to say to God the Father at the end of His life on earth, "I have finished the works you gave me to do."

For this group, relationship with God is based primarily in knowing about Him on an intellectual level. It is to know what He wants them to do and doing it. Their key life principle is: "If you know more, you will live a better life." They are frequently heard saying, "I know that; I can do that." Or on the other side of the same coin, "I will never do that again," only to find themselves repenting of it again later.

The second group of people are those who desire to know the Lord God on His terms. These are people who recognize the limitations of their best human attempts to know and please God. These are people who seek to know their works for God will never be good enough to merit His blessing. For these people, the real issues are those of their own hearts. These people seek to know Him personally and intimately by faith. They are people who experience His love and grace personally. They are people who are apprehended by His loving heart of grace and mercy—love and mercy they know they don't deserve.

> **No person, by human grit or determination, can serve God acceptably.**

The issue of living a life that is pleasing to God is to embrace a broken and contrite heart, to confess the inner need of the Lord's presence and power, and to offer one's self to Him, choosing passion for His ways. These people's axiom is: If you know Him and choose to love Him you will walk in His ways. The only feasible motivation to obedience is loving God with all your heart, soul, mind, and strength.

People such as these found in Scripture, have a tremendous foundation stone. They chose as their basic understanding, a principle it has taken me a long time to grasp, but which I want to invest the rest of my life trying to understand and teach others. It is the principle of motivation summed up this way: *the love of God can keep you where human effort or duty can't even take you!*

Please allow me to give you just one biblical example of the two different ways people chose to walk in God's blessing in life. Adam and Eve had two sons: Cain and Abel. You can read their story in Genesis chapter 4. Permit me to give you the "Revised Hepner Edition" of that chapter.

Cain was a farmer who brought to God the crops he had grown and asked God to bless that offering. He was, in essence, telling the Lord this was the best he could do, and he wanted to find God's acceptance on that basis. "Lord God, here is my best effort at pleasing you. Bless me."

Abel, on the other hand, asked his dad, Adam, what offering God had accepted when he and his mom, Eve, had fallen into the sin of eating from the Tree of the Knowledge of Good and Evil. His dad told him that God had shed a ram's blood in their place and had covered them with the skins of the animal. Abel had a broken heart and deep humility. He wanted to offer God what would please Him. So, as a shepherd, he took his most prized lamb and shed its blood, asking God to accept this offering in his place.

The Scripture says God looked on Abel's humble and broken-hearted offering with pleasure, but God did not look with favor on Cain's offering of self-effort. The Bible says this made Cain very angry. He had his pride hurt. He thought his brother made him look bad, so he killed his brother in a fit of vengeance. In reality, Cain looked bad because he had a wrong heart and made choices to try to walk in the blessings of God on his own terms! This, in my mind, is a classic illustration of the two different ways people choose to walk in the ways of God.

You have hung in there with me and have joined me in throwing stones at fifteen giants of the heart. The enemy of our souls was using those giants of the heart as obstacles and roadblocks to our walking by faith with the Lord in deepening intimacy with Him. While those giants stood in our hearts, we weren't set free to really see Him in His majesty and splendor. The enemy himself owned small parts of the "ground" of our hearts as we permitted those things to live in us without opposing them. But now that we have attacked them one by one, and have seen them hit the road, we are ready to see something about the Christian life many people never see . . . let alone comprehend and live.

The essence of the Christian life is found in the biblical Immanuel Principle. The essence of Christianity is the miracle of God Almighty, the Holy Spirit, living His life in us. You and I are miracles of grace, the literal habitations of the Lord—sanctuaries of His Spirit! There are two of us living in my body: the Holy Spirit and me. Maturing in our Christian life is not a function of how old we are or how many years we have known Him. Maturing in our relationship with the Lord is simply our choice to cooperate with the Holy Spirit as He formulates the life of Jesus in us! The life in which we are rooted bears fruit in our lives. When we are rooted in Jesus Christ our Lord, He is divine life in us and we bear His fruit.

> **The essence of Christianity is the miracle of God Almighty, the Holy Spirit, living His life in us.**

Listen carefully as your inner counselor, the Holy Spirit, teaches you the truth regarding the supernatural nature of the Christian life. Permit the Spirit of God to make the following Scriptures come alive to you:

> I will ask the Father, and *he will give you another Counselor to be with you forever*—the Spirit of Truth. The world cannot accept him, because it neither sees him nor knows him. But you will know him, for he lives with you and will be in you. I will not leave you as orphans: *I will come to you. Before long the world will not see me anymore, but you will see me.* Because I live you also will live. On that day you will realize that I am in my Father and *you are in me and I am in you.* Whoever has my commands and obeys them is the one who loves me. He who loves me will be loved by my Father, and *I too will love him and show myself to him.* (John 14:16–21, emphasis mine)

> My dear children for whom I am again in the pains of childbirth, *until Christ is formed in you.* (Gal. 4:19, emphasis mine)

> For we who are alive are always being given over to death for Jesus' sake, *so that His life may be revealed in our mortal body.* (2 Cor. 4:11, emphasis mine)

The powerful truth of the matter is that there is no one on earth who can live a successful and meaningful Christian life. The Christian life, in the biblical sense, is becoming like Christ. The Greek word *christianos* literally means "ones who are like Christ" or "little Christs." No amount of human striving will ever accomplish our becoming like Christ. We cannot emulate Him nor walk in His ways, regardless of our degree of effort. The simple fact is that God must live the Christian life in us by the Holy Spirit. The biblical principle is: *only Jesus can be Jesus in me.* The sooner we learn that fact and come to the end of our efforts to do it our way, the sooner His Spirit can raise up His image in us!

The fifteen giants of the heart we have studied, attacked, and defeated one at a time, stood in direct opposition to the Spirit of God's desire to raise up the image of Jesus in us. These inner issues were enemy-occupied territory. They were either entry points, footholds, or strongholds in which the enemy of our soul worked. Every time we have defeated an internal giant we have removed a place for the enemy to stand, and we have given more room in our hearts for the Holy Spirit to stand. In the process, we have experienced a corresponding advance of the Kingdom of God in our hearts. As we give Him place to stand, He leads us to the altar of God. The more we learn to know Him, the more we desire of Him. He leads us in passionate longing for more of His gracious presence in our lives. I am set free to go on offering myself to God daily as a living sacrifice, wholly given to Him, which is my only fitting act of worship to the Lord God.

You have done a great job of deciding to stick with me and be an overcomer in your own heart and life. To be an overcomer in life requires that we are first more than conquerors in our own hearts and lives; then "our hearts do not condemn us" when we step out in faith to walk with God. I am so happy for your deeper surrender to the Lord God. He reigns in more areas of your life than ever before. I must give you one more piece of counsel before we close out this book. One last biblical principle to build on is that the enemy will try to retake ground. Satan and his evil beings are not going to just roll over and leave you alone. The enemy hates to lose ground in the lives of people through the works of the Lord Jesus Christ. Expect counterattacks and the second wave of the offensive. He will, in fact, seek to establish in your heart the garbage you have taken to the cross and have seen crucified with Christ. So please understand this truth:

The Ground We Have Gained in Prayer Must Be Maintained in Prayer

You have been set free to walk with God in more profound ways. The Lord delights in your two-way conversations together. Don't neglect these times of deep, personal, and intimate prayer with Him. Take the time to allow His Spirit to do His refreshing and restoring works in your heart regularly. The Lord loves you and is passionate about the ground you have surrendered to His heart. He is your rock and shield, your defender and fortress. Keep bringing to Him—daily or more often if necessary—the issues of your life with which you may be struggling.

I close with a favorite passage of Scripture the Lord gave to me when I was walking in some very dark days of personal trial by fire. They are found in an obscure little book of prophecy in the Old Testament—Zephaniah 3:14–17. Please allow the Holy Spirit to make them personal to your heart and life too:

> Sing, O Daughter of Zion; shout aloud, O Israel! Be glad and rejoice with all your heart, O Daughter of Jerusalem! The Lord has taken away your punishment, he has turned back your enemy. The Lord, the King of Israel, is with you; never again will you fear any harm. On that day they will say to Jerusalem, "Do not fear, O Zion; do not let your hands hang limp. The Lord your God is

with you, he is mighty to save. He will take great delight in you, he will quiet you with his love, he will rejoice over you with singing."

My fellow giant-slayer, do you hear soft heavenly music in your heart?

To order additional copies of

send $14.00 plus 3.95 shipping and handling to

Books, Etc.
PO Box 1406
Mukilteo, WA 98275

or have your credit card ready and call

(800) 917-BOOK